Broken Wing, Falling Sky

Broken Wing, Falling Sky

Fran Muir

TURNSTONE PRESS

Turnstone Press
Artspace Building
018-100 Arthur Street
Winnipeg, MB
R3B 1H3 Canada
www.TurnstonePress.com

Turnstone Press gratefully acknowledges the assistance of the Canada Council for
the Arts, the Manitoba Arts Council, the Government of Canada through the Book
Publishing Industry Development Program, and the Government of Manitoba
through the Department of Culture, Heritage and Tourism, Arts Branch, for our
publishing activities.

Certain portions of this book have been published previously in other forms:
Young Bloods, Stories from Exile 1972-2001, Exile Editions, 2001, *A Line Below
The Skin*, Turnstone Press, 2001, *Coming to Bone,* Exile Editions, 1997, and in the
journals *Exile The Literary Quarterly*, 1998, *Canadian Woman's Studies*, Spring/
Summer, 1995, and *Tessera*, Summer, 1995.

Cover design: Jamis Paulson
Interior design: Sharon Caseburg
Printed and bound in Canada by Hignell for Turnstone Press.

Library and Archives Canada Cataloguing in Publication

Muir, Fran
    Broken wing, falling sky / Fran Muir.

ISBN 978-0-88801-331-6

    1. Muir, Fran 2. Medical care—Canada. 3. Mothers and daughters.
4. Authors, Canadian (English)—20th century—

Biography. I. Title.

PS8576.U338B76 2008   C813'.54   C2008-901421-9

For Jean

Her Grandchildren

And Great-grandchildren

Acknowledgements

I am grateful for the encouragement and support I received from my family and from friends, both during the events this book describes, and in the aftermath, and the invaluable assistance given to me during the writing of this work.

Jeannie Lochrie, Tracy Lynch, Connie Chisholm, and Jan Barnsley read through the early drafts. Their insights kept me tracking essentials, as did my editors, Barbara Kuhne, and Pat Sanders, my editor at Turnstone Press, as they guided this work to its eventual shape.

During the course of searching family history, many archivists and librarians and others gave vital assistance, both in Britain and Canada. Although acknowledged in a previous publication, it is important to mention again here the kindness and generosity of those at my mother's place of birth, and the help they provided.

My thanks, with appreciation, go to Turnstone Press for bringing *Broken Wing, Falling Sky* to publication.

Author's Note

In this memoir, fragments of memory, family history, and journal entries have been interwoven with medical and other records obtained under freedom of information legislation. These records will appear throughout the book in italicized form. Quotation marks denote actual words spoken or reproduced from other sources.

Sources for pharmaceutical information and other related notes are contained in an appendix.

Broken Wing, Falling Sky

August 5, 1998, Vancouver, BC I am gazing into a bowl of golden light lying below very blue mountains. The Lions look down from across the bowl, onto tops of trees climbing from Pacific Ocean to the park where my mother Jean's linden tree has put out its third year of leaves and delicately scented creamy yellow blossoms. Summer clouds feather outspread wings across the sky and I am falling. Falling into memory's river, fast running and full of rocks the colour of flesh, water the colour of light.

My mother died in late September 1994. She was ninety. Born New Year's Day, 1904, into an ungentle world, and when Jean died she did not go gently, nor was my watching her slip through a crack in time gentle. The fall of her passing was fittingly as luminous as those brilliant Indian summers of her native Manitoba, hers and mine; as is the gift I received of beginning to know, as I had never known, the woman who was my mother, in the midst of tragic circumstances, of her abuse with anti-psychotic drugs that finally ended the life of a fiercely independent woman. Luminous in me is the woman I met, finally, when she was facing an aggressive world that increasingly would not accommodate an *old woman* whose mind was breaking loose from Aristotelian logic, that cornerstone of rationality, to be simply who she was, her memory floating like a leaf, landing where it would. Is this the way it should be? No ends middles beginnings, but floating unbound, spiralling into earth, sky. She is still here in the spaces of the house that is my mind, cells of my body, chambers of my heart, as the memories form to absorb her, and from her, into what I wish to keep, yet slipping as though water through my fingers. Where is the beginning? How to write the remembered silences of our life together, what was never said; carried, but never spoken?

Jean and her daughter, Fran.

Islands in a Gap

"Your mother's heart fibrillated under anaesthesia," one of the doctors across from me said. There were two of them, young residents dressed in green fatigues. I noticed their eyes, wary, watching me. Between us, my mother, Jean, her left breast cut away, lay silent under neatly folded sheets.

Earlier that month, June 1988, I told my mother I was divorcing after thirty years of marriage. Her hand was on her belly when she told me I "must be crazy," adding, "it can be very hard, being alone." She appeared distraught. I had no memory of hearing the word *lonely* come from her lips. At that moment, she also had something she needed to tell me. She had found a small lump in her breast, would be going in for a lumpectomy, was all she said, other than I was not to bother her doctors, afraid I might offend them and this might affect "how they treat me on the operating table." When we lived in northern British Columbia some years before, Jean phoned me from Vancouver, in the midst of an acute attack of glaucoma. She was being taken to Emergency. The eye specialist who performed emergency treatment to release pressure in her eyes (and who had treated her ever since) was angry with her because I had called him long distance to find out what her situation was, called him at his home number volunteered by hospital staff.

I looked across my mother, at those restless-to-move-on young doctors in their green uniforms. Yes ...? my look said, waiting for more. "The good news is we got it all, no further treatment needed," the quick response from one of them, their eyes still watching me for mine. A lumpectomy, was this all she was told, or all she told me? Something, a small pause in me, a still point in which I calibrated the spaces between words, the opacity of their eyes, that in hindsight became the sense they knew something that I, we, did not. They were wanting me to believe in their success. *Her* irregular heart, these residents seemed to be telling me, in a moment that felt out of time, the consequences of whatever had happened belonged to her, would require Jean to take digoxin for the rest of her life, her daily bread. I questioned side effects. "There aren't any," what they said. I sensed their carefulness. "As long as her blood levels are monitored," they added casually. I realized they didn't know, or weren't saying.

Fibrillation, a rapid series of contractions of the heart, unsteady, irregular, broken, discontinuous, erratic, wild ... that morning Jean was draped for surgery, the offending breast exposed, no longer hers. Eradication of her breast required that all of Jean's natural defences, her mind, consciousness, and sense of pain, her memory and her muscles be disabled by a combination of drugs in a general anaesthesia, to achieve loss of consciousness, amnesia, analgesia, and muscle relaxation. Some twenty minutes into this balancing act, something happened, Jean's heart raced, lost its rhythm. What had gone wrong? Most general anaesthetics are potent heart muscle depressants and dilate blood vessels. They are metabolized by older patients with less efficiency, which will affect what is a safe dosage for someone who is over sixty years of age. For older patients, the risks associated with anaesthesia are greater, their reactions to drugs more complex and individualistic. Jean's anaesthetist, for this mastectomy, wrote in her records, prior to her surgery, that she was in good health, on no medications and had a normal electrocardiogram. He left a cryptic query: *respiratory problem with general anaesthesis?* Was he aware that four years earlier at this same hospital, when Jean had surgery to remove a cataract, her records from that time indicated she did have a respiratory problem with inhalant anaesthesia? Her anaesthetist at that time (1984) indicated this method of general anaesthesia was not an appropriate option for her, and proceeded at that time with a local combined anaesthetic. Did the anaesthetist for her mastectomy now, in 1988, consult these records? Or was his abbreviated note questioning the accuracy of information Jean may have given about herself?

Jean's surgeon noted in her records that *breast cancer in elderly women such as this are best treated with total mastectomy and low axillary dissection,* that he had discussed this with Jean and she was in agreement with this. I have no way of knowing, now, and did not know then, what Jean's unspoken doubts and fears, or wishes, may have been, whether she repressed them in the overwhelm of what she was being told, or whether any other options were mentioned or available to her at that time. The Cancer Control Agency of British Columbia indicated that in 1988 there was a surgical alternative to the modified radical mastectomy carried out on Jean. It is referred to in their literature as a wide lumpectomy, considered appropriate where the tumour is less than 4 cm and singly focused, a procedure that can be done with local rather than inhalant anaesthesia. In this procedure, the tumour and a safety zone of surrounding normal tissue is removed along with some or all of the neighbouring lymph nodes, which are then tested for any signs of invading cancer cells. Jean's lymph nodes, removed along with her breast in the modified radical mastectomy, showed no signs of malignancy. Options, and how "going in for a lumpectomy" turned into a radical modified mastectomy done under inhalant anaesthesia, was something Jean never discussed with me, nor did I feel I could ask.

Jean seemed very confused in the first days after the mastectomy. I mentioned this to the nurses and the surgical resident, who made a note in her chart that she was *more* confused and forgetful. I wondered, upon reading this later, if he assumed this was the natural state of an older woman. I explained to staff then that I had never known Jean to be confused or forgetful. This resident then suggested that it was likely secondary to anaesthesia or the hospital environment and should clear up on its own. A cardiologist, called in when Jean's heart fibrillated, stated in her records he could find no reason for this event, and attributed it to a pre-existing condition. However, there were no symptoms at any time prior to her surgery and none indicated on her pre-op electrocardiogram, as her anaesthetist had noted. Another source of disturbed heart rhythm, this cardiologist did not mention in Jean's records, which medical and pharmaceutical literature does indicate, is that atrial irritation can be caused by the inhalation of toxic gases and drugs that disturb the heartbeat or even cause permanent damage to the heart muscle, such as those administered to Jean before and during her surgery. Early signs of possible drug-induced harm went unacknowledged in Jean's medical records.

Hospital nursing notes over the immediate post-op recovery period after her mastectomy indicated Jean was, variously, *comfortable, no complaints, rhythm normal, slightly disoriented but knows where she is, stable and settled, ambulatory, confused at times, oriented in all 3 spheres, no confusion noted, denies incisional discomfort, no voiced complaints, refused analgesic, up in her chair most of the day.* A physiotherapist during this same period, prior to Jean's discharge from hospital observed: *an independent homemaker, lives alone, walks 4-5 blocks a day, alert and cooperative, good historian, oriented x3 but vague with some answers, requires supervision when ambulating due to her dream-like state, remains vague and in a 'trance-like' state at times when she is walking....*

Light on an Outspread Wing

Jean's *lazy eye* escaped detection in childhood. With minimal vision in that eye, Jean worked all her adult life at bookkeeping jobs, for the air force during World War II and, after, with a small airline that transported materials and people into northern Canada. She left Winnipeg in 1970 when she was "retired" without pension after twenty-four years working for this company, moved to Vancouver and began working again for Office Overload at various office jobs until she was seventy-nine, stopped only by the combination of economic recession cutbacks in the early 1980s and threatening loss of vision, this time from cataracts.

In spite of failing eyesight, Jean walked every day, a lifetime habit that now replaced her other lifetime rhythm of going out to work. I was living with my family in northern BC and had no idea how close to blindness Jean had come, until we invited her to accompany my husband and me to visit Winnipeg, on part of our holiday trip east. In Winnipeg, along streets in noticeable disrepair, Jean stumbled, a lot, almost falling several times: a strong, tall, erect woman, independent, unable to hide her inability to make her way through broken-down streets of what used to be home. She was eighty. I hid my alarm, until the day before her return to Vancouver, when my husband and I would carry on to Montreal. This was when she mentioned, for the first time, that on her return to Vancouver she was scheduled for eye surgery to have a lens implant, that for the last several years glaucoma had been complicating her need for this surgery to restore vision in her "good eye." Jean was, again, very clear I was not to get involved, or speak to her doctor, not even come to the hospital to visit her.

I did, changing my return ticket. I expected Jean would not be pleased to see me. She was, noticeably, even enthusiastic greeting me when I arrived, her doctors and the hospital staff informed by her that her "daughter is here now," so she "can go home." Staff there seemed relieved to release her to me—someone's rescuer, I felt, although not sure whose, so noticeable was the alacrity with which she was suddenly discharged to a home that required intensive organizing so she would be able to spend the next couple of months without bending or lifting. Hospital records from this time would later reveal that, even at this earlier time, Jean was exposed to an inappropriate medication, Stemetil. The lens implant a success, we left the hospital, innocence beguiled by a notion of restored freedom. Jean managed on her own; her sight, her physician told her, was now at the minimum required to drive a car. Jean expressed deceptively quiet pleasure at being able to see the mountains again, and flowers. She had never learned to drive a car.

Aside from this 1984 cataract surgery and previous glaucoma, acute in its onset, requiring two surgical procedures during the 1970s, Jean had good health. A surgery to correct bunions when she was younger was the only other time Jean had ever been in hospital. To my knowledge she had no other serious or chronic illness, a bronchitis one winter several years ago. She mentioned once there might be a slight emphysema, which, she had been advised, was likely genetic. Physically strong and resilient, her physical appearance belied her age, which in the long run may have worked against her.

June 25, 1988, I was again accompanying Jean out of hospital, having been told ... what had we been told? What did either of us know? I was left wondering why so much was gone, her whole left breast, how many lymph nodes? There would be no follow-up chemotherapy, or radiation. I was left wondering if it was cancer, Jean never spoke of it. I felt silenced by her silence. A week later at her follow-up appointment, her surgeon avoided my eyes when he called her into his office. I was torn between wanting to be in there with her, to ask questions, wondering if she would, and respecting her privacy, knowing I was "not to bother her doctors." About this she had continued to be very clear. It would remain to Jean and to me to discover, each in our own way, what the *successful* amputation of her breast meant, what her hospital records did not acknowledge; the meaning of those spaces between words. Right then there was only altered vision, an absent breast, and a heart underneath that had gone momentarily erratic ... wild, and my growing awareness of a sense of much gone missing.

Jean's fear of doctors' anger and what they might do to her seemed at odds with the person I knew as my mother. It raised a question in me—why didn't we, I, question her doctors; why did I not ask my mother more? Respect for her wishes? Yes, of course, but the silence between us had resonated more, something that felt childlike in me. I was just moving myself and our dog out of what had been our family home, to an older, subdivided house, where I had rented space, no more than ten minutes by car from where Jean had lived since she'd come to Vancouver. My three children were adults, my daughter, recently married and living in Vancouver, my sons working in eastern Canada. My history with this woman who was my mother had been conflicted, complicated, lay like that vast prairie landscape, that sea of grasses sighing, weeping, that ocean my grandmother Jane crossed, to an unknown future on a prairie homestead, giving birth to my mother Jean, called Jane at her birth, New Year's Day, 1904, after having birthed ten sons; each of us swimming our own natal sea.

Jean revealed little, of joy or distress. Silent about her past, and my father's as well, after his sudden death when I was eleven. Ironic perhaps, that he was a history teacher. She remained a widow throughout the remainder of her life. I had constructed my mother from a child's world, from memory's selections and censorings, images like photographic negatives looking for light, an undersong of call for response, for the difference between expectation and what it is that gives pause, resonates with what has not yet been taken into account. I found my adult self searching for an absent father in all my writing. It would be in these last years of Jean's life, when I finally became aware of the search for her as well, that I began to feel her breath in me, and his, and ultimately, my own ... discovering many are the presumptions woven from an absence of knowing.

Sea of Grass

Although Jean dissuaded me from ever considering becoming a teacher, she remained proud of what my father did, telling me at some point that he was a good teacher and that his students won prizes in provincial exams. Her preoccupation with my getting a "good" education meant going to university. She was respectful of those who had—too much so, I remember thinking, feeling the weight of her expectations for me, something I did not and could not recognize as a reflection of her feelings about herself, her history, unknown to me then. As a child and young woman, I experienced but did not understand the source of what was displaced on to me, her only child, of what people would think, of having a good job, being self-supporting, surviving poverty, as she eked out a living for us both from a minute income from office bookkeeping. I didn't know, then, that she had been a teacher too, before she met my father, in small country schools in isolated prairie communities bound by strictures of attitude, religious or otherwise; that when her father died, any possibility of her going to university ended.

Jean had grown up on a farm, that I had known at some point, although she had rarely spoken about it. I knew there were some uncles—I had met one, and spent a few weeks on his farm when I was ten. I did not know that Jean had ten brothers, that she was the eleventh and youngest child. She would tell me later that, growing up on that prairie homestead, her mother had given her freedom to roam; her brothers didn't think she helped enough with the chores. Jean was a graceful and elegant woman, taller than my father, who was slight of build, light of weight. I was an absent-minded, daydreaming child, awkward, skinny, and messy, bit my nails, wrote clumsily with my left hand, did nothing, it seemed to me, neatly, or well. Jean never commented on any of this, other than encouraging me to try not to bite my nails. Her elegant taste combined with lack of money led Jean to shop selectively for clothing. I was bored and balked at the time spent with her in this pursuit, developed a long-lasting impatience with shopping, was happiest roaming down by the Assiniboine River, and through vacant lots filled with hints of wildness: fox tails, burrs, thistles, cheery dandelions, crickets, cheeky grasshoppers, and when early spring's skin of ice was ready for cracking, seeing how deep I could wade before my boots filled with snow melt. Jean was perhaps perplexed and bewildered by this child of hers. My spaces were city streets and back lanes with their giant hollyhock faces peering over fences or springing up from underneath them, rioting to get out, it seemed, and where horses pulled wagons delivering milk, bread, ice, parcels from Eaton's and Hudson's Bay, and stood patiently in hot summer sun, in their straw hats with holes cut for their twitching ears, munching in oat bags, if it was that time, switching their tails against a myriad of flies. I knew without touching that their muzzles would be velvet. Their eyes behind the longest lashes I had ever seen, when they looked down at me from around blinders that were put on to keep them from shying, were very large and seemed to hold the world. Our income provided for few opportunities—church groups where you had to do handwork, I hated, because I felt clumsy, uncoordinated, and my hands got wet with sweat and messed everything up. Instead, I often skipped, and took my collection money downtown to movie theatres on Portage Avenue. There were times a streetcar conductor looked the other way when all I had was a penny to put in the token box, coming home too late for girls my age to be downtown by themselves. My mother didn't know. If she had, it wouldn't have happened.

As Jean's heart went wild on the operating table that day in June,

1988, and beat through its hidden chambers, the right and left atria, from the Latin *atrium,* meaning *corridor,* and the right and left ventricle, from the Latin *ventriculus,* meaning a little belly, the electrocardiogram picked up extremely rapid, random, irregular impulses through the atria corridors, which triggered in the little bellies, the ventricles, an irregular pattern of many weak squeezes, reducing the vital flow of breath-filled blood to her body, which signalled her heart to speed up even more. The river of blood flowing through Jean's body could pool in the atria, debris clots, if formed here, could, if carried downstream, lodge, for example, in her brain, cutting off access to her navigational aids, retrieval of what happened yesterday, last week, an hour ago, names of things; her name, location in time, space. The heart is its own pacemaker—the more life fills the heart, the harder the heart works. Where is the heart's mind?

Digoxin, a cardiac glycoside, which Jean had been told to take every day for the rest of her life, works to slow the heart rate by slowing nerve impulses through the heart muscle and making the ventricular contractions stronger, increasing blood volume output, therefore providing more oxygen to the body. Digoxin is also a drug that can become toxic if its blood level is too high for the person taking it, and disturb the heart's beat, causing permanent damage, producing the irregular heartbeat symptoms this drug is meant to control. It can also, in its physiological effect, mimic symptoms of a loss of mental faculties; affecting memory, producing confusional and other states which can then be mistaken for psychosis. The range between a therapeutic and a toxic dose of digoxin is described as so narrow that careful and frequent monitoring of blood levels of digoxin is required. Aging and individual sensitivity are further risks, for even if a person's blood levels are within the "accepted normal range," the dosage could still be toxic for that individual, for Jean. June 1988, what Jean may have been told about these risks by her surgeon or her regular physician remained unknown to me ... "no side effects," the residents in their greens told me across the bed where Jean lay silent.

Over the summer of 1988, Jean appeared to recover well from the mastectomy. She did her exercises, regained the use of her left arm with no apparent complications, other than that she would always need to be very careful of any cut or scratch on this arm or hand, because lymph nodes had been removed. So independent, she did not take kindly to suggestions she might need help. We had never spent much time together in the years since I left home in the late fifties, leaving Winnipeg for Toronto right after graduating from University of Manitoba, with the person who would became my husband for thirty years, at this time knowing practically nothing of Jean's history, and little of mine—I don't recall asking many questions from across the unexplored territory between us. I did not tell Jean I had found a job in Toronto until I was on the verge of leaving. This, because I was afraid she would find out my boyfriend and future husband was going with me. He had finished his courses the year before, waited around in Winnipeg for me to complete the fifth year of my science degree, so we could leave together, and he would look for work, once in Toronto. Later, I discovered Jean had pretty much assumed we were leaving together. My boyfriend's family were evangelical Christians. Jean had become uncharacteristically antagonistic. Neither Jean nor my father ever spoke out against religions or religious faith. They were, as far as I knew, agnostic and not church-going, although Jean sent me to Sunday school at the church around the corner. At that time, when I was eighteen, nineteen, twenty ... I needed to know there was love in the world, had discovered the gospels, particularly St. John's words, *Set your troubled hearts at rest ... in my Father's house are many dwelling places, if it were not so I should have told you ... I am the good shepherd ... and lay down my life for the sheep ...* and that evangelical Christians believed this with a fervour. Much, much later, the natural world that had befriended me as a child would receive me again, become a home, the place to which I would one day return, when I went back to where I had come from—until then, I would call myself a secular humanist, if anyone asked, and respect this mystery that life is. Looking back to that time of leave-taking, I realized it was not my boyfriend himself, of whom Jean said later she had always liked, nor his beliefs per se, but that she believed it could lead me into fanaticism, hypocrisy, and anti-intellectualism. I had confused these concerns with criticism and rejection of me; essentially, it was that she feared I would be derailed from becoming self-supporting and independent. She wanted more for me than what she had achieved for herself. But back then, in my late teens and early twenties, what I felt was a gulf between us, ever-widening, and Jean's disapproval of who I thought I was. When later I quit my job, giving up that university training to stay home full time and raise a family, became a suburban mom, the gulf seemed even wider, at least in my mind. I took great joy in my family, three children by then, and had begun to experience feelings of having been too much on my own through my own childhood, and that I didn't seem prepared in any way to fit in as a suburban housewife, or anywhere else. There was frustration, anger, and a feeling of needing to alienate myself from my past. I did not, could not see then, or appreciate, what Jean had given me. Her grandchildren made their own bridges to her, and she to them. My connection to Jean was never broken, by either of us, just weighed down with what remained unspoken.

Jean did not come to the train station with me when I left for Toronto. Although I'd waited until just after finishing final exams to tell her I had been offered a job in Toronto, and I was leaving almost immediately, she seemed pleased when I gave her my news. She was busy scrubbing kitchen cupboards as the taxi arrived. I began, awkwardly, to say goodbye, upset at her preoccupation with the cupboards, and heard her say, "You will come back sometime, won't you ...?" her words a shock, disconcerting uncertainty there in her voice, as though in a moment we had changed places ... *of course* was about all I could find to say. Whatever I felt at that moment mingled with and complicated the sense of release, lightness, and freedom growing in me as I began my life in Toronto. The last time I remembered hugging Jean, or being hugged by her, I was small enough that my arms wrapped around her legs, and, looking up at her, had asked why she couldn't stay home with me. Bending over with her arms around me and lifting me up a little off my feet, she smiled down at me and told me I wasn't enough to stay home for, not unkindly, nor with impatience; telling it like it was. Were these her words, or what the child felt?

As the summer of 1988 progressed, Jean and I said little about my divorce. No longer a wife, my children leading adult lives, I was preoccupied with setting up a home for myself with our family dog, a wonky but dear golden retriever we called Samantha, Sam, who came to us as a very small puppy newly separated from her birth family, when my own children were completing high school and leaving home for college. This summer, in contrast to her former bumptious golden retriever friendliness, Sam's manner altered when she was with Jean. Had her animal radar picked up some clue from Jean? I see them in my mind, now—we are out for drives, Sam sitting erect on the back seat of the car, gazing ahead, queen-like; Jean erect in the passenger seat, both in what I can only describe as a relationship of mutual awareness, respectful restraint, until Sam died, two years before Jean. Sam missed all our children when they left home, and continued to wait for them to return, in all her usual places, until, eventually, she stopped. It had made sense that I would take Sam with me after the divorce, but life is never so simple. That summer Sam chewed to pieces the metal licence attached to her collar, still around her neck, when she heard my former husband's voice on my answering machine.

I had, while living in northern BC, and since coming to Vancouver, been writing short fiction and some poetry; some of it had, or was being published, and I'd begun working at completing a degree in English literature, taking credit courses by correspondence from the University of BC. When we first arrived in Vancouver, complications from a previous back surgery flared up and became fairly incapacitating for a year or more, but when my back had settled down somewhat, I began attending some night courses on campus at UBC. Now, with a single life ahead of me, I needed to make some decisions about what I would do next, and decided to return to university, part-time that fall and winter of 1988, uneasy as to how my back would hold up with all that sitting. Initially this return to classes was stressful. I found myself incredibly self-conscious, slipping early into the back of class, avoiding student cafeterias, and sensitive to what I perceived as my "mature and divorced" status. Did I really belong here? Gradually I made some friendships, one in particular, someone I had met during the night course I had attended the previous winter, before Jean's mastectomy, my divorce. We had reconnected over the summer and found we were close neighbours, and often took Sam to the woods for long walks on a Saturday or Sunday morning. My children couldn't have been more supportive, keeping in touch and encouraging me in what I was attempting to do in my life. As fall turned to winter, life had begun to take on some rhythmic familiarity; exams, a welcome Christmas break, dinner at my newly married daughter and son-in-law's apartment, with Jean, and a few of their young friends, with whom Jean seemed to get along well in conversation, although I sensed an unease in her, which, at one level, I related to her reserve, the privacy of her emotions and feelings, but I also felt my own unease, felt it responding to something more inchoate. We celebrated her eighty-sixth birthday at New Years'. My daughter and her husband had been out of the country travelling the previous year, and were now living not far from Jean and myself, here in Vancouver, and would soon be preparing for another year away, this time in West Africa, living and working there for some months.

Winter moved toward spring, and at least a temporary end to the now familiar routines of being a student with classes to attend ... Anthropology, Drama, Chaucer, Commonwealth Literature; term papers ... "Construction," one professor told me. "You need construction." I write fiction, I told him. "You live in an Aristotelian world," he told me; "things have a beginning, middle, and end." The last time I had been on my own, or felt it, was as a child, Jean's daughter. I was feeling the weight of what that might mean. Did the beginning hold the end; the end, the beginning? Where was the middle? Where was I?

Still Jean's daughter, I wrote in my journal, *memories close as breathing, that have been lying in reserve, seemingly quiescent, are slipping from amnesia as myriad resistant threads of our mutuality of mouth teeth throat belly eye ear doubling through the four chambers of a heart born of our vanishings, speaking with a language the shape of heart breath, in a voice of erasure too close to the skin....* The words on my journal pages changed shape from small and cramped to large, illegible scrawling across spaces between lines and into child-like rhythms and modulations, traced a return to before that felt like something coming to meet me head-on.

Goodbye Aristotle

Tiny feet, mine, pad over cold linoleum, patches of frost there bite toes, frozen water pump at the kitchen sink, coal oil lamp making winter morning shadows, my father, not my mother, laying a fire in the wood stove ... memory taking me out of time, a small child again, or still.

They called it jaundice then. Jean referred to it later as the time when she "ate a lot of Lily White corn syrup." My father must have fixed breakfast for his toddler and his ailing wife, before going to school. This was a Manitoba hamlet a few hundred miles north of Winnipeg, almost on the border with Saskatchewan, where my father was principal of a consolidated school. Student were brought in from outlying districts by horse-driven, wooden school vans that waited to return the children home, winter smoke curling from their chimneys, horses' breath turning vans and horses to ghostly hoarfrost shapes by early dark of winter afternoons. Jean had told me my father taught literature and history to grade eleven and twelve students.

A large snake in our backyard, back there, I am probably three, transfixed by its skin glowing hypnotic patterns the colour of fear;

tasting it. Neither of us moves. Where is my mother? I see her there telling me just before my nap that my father said I shouldn't be afraid of snakes. The child noticing and wondering why my mother doesn't say it herself; know much later how Jean feared snakes, her telling me, with a shiver, of how snakes would raise themselves up and look around in her father's fields of wheat, oats, barley, sending her running out of the fields and into the house. My mother told me the truth—it was my father who said I should not be afraid of snakes. He later found me standing under a horse being shod at the local blacksmith's, took my hand and led me away. I remember telling him, you said not to be afraid, and him telling me that's not what he meant. I don't remember fearing the horse, or him.

I am climbing more stairs than I can count to where my father is teaching his class. I am four, sent by my mother to deliver a message to him. The school is very tall. Taller still the grain elevator and its too long shadow out by railway tracks that would soon take us away from there, along with many of the boys my father taught, on their way to war in Europe. A lot of grinning faces looking at me and my father smiling down at me as I sidle behind his desk, to get away from the grins. My voice curls up inside me, mute. Did I deliver the message—I don't know.

When Jean was born, Einstein was imagining what it would be like to ride on a beam of light. He discovered for us that motion, time, and space are relative, close relatives, conjoined, so to speak, our universe much bigger than we thought, our sun much further from the eye of our spiralling milky way, that gravity bends light. Radio, the telephone, automobiles, and aeroplanes were just becoming, as was an unsettled modern age restless with possibilities released by loss of certainties. By the time Jean was sixteen, women in Britain, Canada, and America had won her the right to vote when she came of age. Several of her brothers had gone and returned from World War I, her brother Frank with his lungs damaged by chlorine gas. My father, too, had returned from that war. By the time Jean and my father married, both their fathers had died, leaving their mothers in poverty. Two years before, the stock market had crashed, drought was turning prairie soil to dust blowing on the wind; the Great Depression was taking hold. When Jean gave birth to me, and another planet was discovered, there was some doubt as to whether one plus one equals two is as straightforward as it seems, and Amelia Earhart had grown wings. When I was two,

Amelia and her wings disappeared from one part of the sky; in another, bombs rained into the sleepy, unaware afternoon of a small town in northern Spain—Picasso told the story in *Guernica*. Jean's mother, my grandmother, Jane died; a year later, Kristallnacht, the shattering clear as glass in Germany. Another war was coming.

With the war on, Jean took me, left that little hamlet where my life began, left it one spring, when I was five, taking me with her on the train, to look for full-time work in Winnipeg. My father would join us when the school year was over. We stayed, initially, at the YWCA, until Jean found a boarding house, and left me with the woman who ran it while she job hunted. All I remember of that time was an afternoon filled with wailing fire sirens, huge plumes of smoke in the sky, the landlady telling me there was a big fire downtown; my mother hadn't come home. Gravity distorts time, motion, space, bends light in a small child, until her mother's reappearance. Jean had found a job bookkeeping "for the air force," she told me. My father would teach young recruits, high school boys heading overseas to Europe and the War, at Camp Shilo, an army camp west of Winnipeg, near Brandon. He disappeared from my life then, to return from time to time on some weekends, for the duration of the war. My father, then almost fifty, had been a sniper in France during the final months of the First World War, Jean told me when I was about the age he was at my birth.

Where was home? We came to rooms in a converted office building, with a gas stove, no running water, no closets, a bathroom down the hall, and an army of cockroaches on manoeuvres from the fish and chip shop downstairs. I watched their progress down across the wall above the stove, from an army camp cot Jean had set up for me in the room designated as kitchen. Several applications of plaster to the corners where walls met ceiling minimized these skin-shivering bug incursions. The street outside, Osborne Street, indifferent, with a life of its own, taking a childish forgetful innocence up into the momentum of a street's existence, the inevitable familiarity of shop windows and streetcars, the baby mice born over the Easter weekend in the bakery's window, gone when the street came to life again after the holiday. Once in school I discovered my mother was not like other mothers. She didn't stay home. There were no aunts, grandparents, close neighbours to watch over her child. A couple of sisters in high school, from a family who lived down the street, walked me to school that first year and took me to their home until Jean got home from her job. After that, I was on my own during the time Jean was at work. Sometime during that first school year I developed chicken pox, found myself in an isolation hospital, in what I remember as a large bare room containing myself, in a crib, and little else but another child, a boy about my age, in another crib in the far corner, who turned my time there into an endless haunting, by taunting me that my parents didn't love me if they put me in this place and must be getting rid of me. He let me know my parents had sent ice cream and grapes for me and these had been given to all of the other children. There were no parental visits allowed. This is all I remember of that time, and that I couldn't ask my parents why they took me there, afraid of what they would tell me. Of course they had no choice, given our circumstances. Where does fear come from? Where does it go?

Only once did I fear my father, but not him, rather the estrangement of his unfamiliar anger, when I went out to play along the back lanes and streets of Winnipeg very early one Sunday morning while he and my mother were still asleep. I was swinging high, feeling bird-like, soaring through an inner spaciousness, on an old swing in the backyard of a run-down boarding house, when he found me, and I discovered a fear in him, when he spanked me then, in public, once, on my bottom, the only time he ever did, had never ever raised his voice. His face was tight and pale—a quiet, patient man who, once riled, I discovered, took time to recover, as I watched him covertly all that day, wanting his company, and, as I often did, to comb his hair as he napped on the couch while listening to Sunday concerts on the radio, to play cribbage with him, and hearts, before he left again for Camp Shilo and the army, until next time.

Jean never once left me alone in the evenings. Saturday mornings were part of her work week, then she shopped. Sunday mornings, when the mothers of my friends were at church, Jean did laundry in the cavernous depths below the building where we had our rooms. A creepy place, reached by going down outside stairs, across a cement courtyard to a doorway by a back lane, and then down dark stairs to a long low stone passageway that opened on a dimly lit space containing a wringer washing machine and scrubbing board, two stone tubs, and lines for hanging the clothes. No windows. A light bulb cast just enough light to barely make out where surrounding rough stone walls began. There were rats scuttling about in storage lockers. Sunday afternoons she baked beans, jam pie, and rice pudding that would last us into the next week, and we had potatoes done in the oven, sometimes with liver, or calf's heart or bacon, and root vegetables. I don't recall my mother cooking hamburgers or things like fresh frozen green peas until my high school years. I remember the radio, run off two large batteries. While my mother ironed on Monday nights we listened to Lux Radio Theatre. During the week there was a continuing drama set on a convoy ship somewhere in the Atlantic, always in imminent danger from a German u boat's torpedo or a marauding air plane. Jean bought our clothing on time payment plans, mine a couple of sizes too big, so I would grow into them. I usually didn't, and when, by junior high school, I was sent home with a note indicating I was underweight, Jean began feeding me bacon and eggs every morning. She never knew I often skipped the breakfasts and lunches she left for me during the week. She even managed a few chocolates as a treat with our Sunday breakfast, and sometimes came home with something exotic, like a pomegranate from the fruit and vegetable store down the street. I still remember sucking on those seeds so compellingly sweet and sour.

I was not a good student. Unhappy in school, restless, inattentive, daydreaming, and careless. I was failing arithmetic in grade four, but a kind teacher who encouraged me, and a promise from Jean of a little signet ring I coveted, in the window of a jeweller's on Osborne Street, if I managed 100 percent in arithmetic by the end of the year, spurred me on to, not 100 percent, but almost, and Jean bought me the ring. It had a tiny diamond chip set in the top and my initials engraved on it. I gave it to my daughter when she went to university. Grade five, a watershed year, the war in Europe, over. Our teacher for that year bullied us, strapped our hands, seemed to take a particular dislike to me, sending me, either to sit underneath her desk, or to the principal's office if I made too many, in her estimation, mistakes in arithmetic. The principal promptly sent me back, which made for a yo-yo kind of existence that year. I don't recall any kind of parent-teacher contact, other than what was written on report cards, or at least not with Jean, who was not home during the day, and I told her nothing of what went on at school, or of how I needed to, and did grow street-wise, very quickly. When I was hospitalized that winter in grade five, with an acute kidney infection, which had emerged with the intensity of appendicitis while I was at school, no one knew how to locate Jean. She finally arrived after some hours and took me by cab to hospital. I lost several weeks of school, and was passed "on trial" at the end of the year. When we were dismissed for the summer holidays and I called Jean at work to tell her of my failure to pass clear, there was only silence on the other end of the phone line. She was disappointed, no doubt worried about me. In need of reassurance she was unable to give me, I got off the phone feeling very alone in my misery—I wasn't good enough for her approval. Due to staff changes, I faced the same teacher for my last year of elementary schooling, unaware then of the assumptions placed upon children who don't come from those neat houses and gardens most of my classmates lived in, but felt it as a growing sense there was something different about me that wasn't as good. My career in smoking and skipping school, developing well by this time, was finally nipped by someone, one of the neighbourhood children, telling me if I was caught smoking I'd be sent to reform school, and Jean's rather brilliant ploy—"your father will be very disappointed ..." which she resorted to on significant occasions, and to long-lasting effect after my father died, as I entered grade seven, when any possibility of disappointing him became enough to shift me almost instantly into high academic gear, no small miracle for either Jean or myself, considering how inattentive and absent-minded I could be. I don't know how Jean managed a bicycle for me, at the end of elementary school, when I did manage to pass clear, a second-hand piano and lessons in grade eight, those summer camps, but she did, without any hint to me of hardship. Even with the odd scholarship, bursary, and summer jobs through my five years of university, it must have been difficult for her to support me at home. One Christmas, she gave me cashmere sweaters she had found on sale at Eaton's. The same three, perhaps four dresses had hung in her cupboard for many years. I see them there in my mind, still.

The summer after graduating from high school, on a trip to Kansas, evidence of racial segregation and an ongoing war in Korea was everywhere—*whites only* signs and men in uniform, duffle bags over their shoulders in all the bus depots. As I headed back to Winnipeg, and was waiting for my connection north in St. Louis, Missouri, I was going up the bus depot escalator behind an African-American woman and her small grandson. She was carrying shopping bags and stumbled as she reached the top, shredding her stocking and cutting her knee. I asked her if there was any way I could help. She looked at me for a moment, as though coming to a decision, then handed me a clean white folded handkerchief and suggested I could wet it for her in the bathroom, which I did, *whites only* posted over the door, bringing it to her and finally attempting to wrap it around her knee. I was pretty awkward. Finally she said, "That's okay, I'll do it." Her small grandson had buried his face against her belly in what I took to be terror. When I sat down to wait for my bus, a white woman walked over to me and said, "You're not from around here, are you." A statement, not a question. I said, no, Canada. "Thought so," she said, "you shouldn't let *them* take advantage of you." I felt relieved to be going home. Jean never spoke about the colour of people's skin, their ethnicity, or race. She was proud of her Scots ancestry. By the time I was in grade nine, we had moved to an apartment in a new building overlooking the Assiniboine River, with running water, a bathroom, electric fridge, and stove—heaven on earth. Set back from a city street and perched on the river's high bank, there were trees of all kinds surrounding us there, filled with more birds than I have seen since. The river bank sloped down to where a small backwater creek formed in spring, early summer, when the river was still high from spring melt, and ducks and turtles had their babies there. Jean had furnished our new home as she could, through sales and on extended time payments. We now had an electric radio with record player. Jean brought home records from time to time—Paul Robeson, Marian Anderson, I knew simply by the wonder of their voices ... the Weavers, Pete Seeger, Dvorak's *New World Symphony*, the Glasgow Orpheus Choir ... others I can't recall, but I do remember hearing this music first in our home.

Memories move as a river breathing with the force of heartbeats unbound, released, unmanageable, undone, wounds not bound up ... a flow of images, music, a murmur, a song for freedom, a cry of anger, loss, or a window suddenly opening, shutting again just as quickly. This would be how Jean and I would go on.

Interlude

Spring, 1989, and a west coast blooming out of drenched rainforest winter, not as it would if, as in Manitoba, winter were a deep thing, but here on this Pacific coast spring is a subtler language of senses and imagination. Tree limbs, branches grow gently softer to the eye, lacier against washed blue air. Light in the forest is green, fresh smells are sweet, real, the trail soft, muddy in low spots. It had been ten months since Jean's breast cancer surgery, my divorce. Euphoria, my classes over, exams to go, when Jean phoned. She did not call me very often, did not chat on the phone. Something unusual in her voice again resonated an uneasiness in me, as she told me she had just received two months' notice of eviction from her apartment. Her home for almost twenty years, since she had moved here from Winnipeg, caught in zoning limbo, as many apartments in her area of Vancouver were. Developers wanted to tear them down and build high-rise condominiums. Older tenants were losing their affordable homes. Protests were taking place in front of bulldozers. Machines prevailed. One of Jean's neighbours, also in her eighties, had a heart attack.

As I wrote my final exams during April, Jean seemed at times, uncharacteristically, paralyzed by confusion and anxiety. When we went to look at apartments for rent, she didn't seem to be able to make up her mind. I was remembering how she had moved to Vancouver from Winnipeg, when she was given sudden notice of "retirement" without a pension, right after her sixty-fifth birthday—she had been with us in northern BC , having flown to Vancouver to accompany me home from there after my back surgery. I don't know if she had received the news before, or after she returned to her home in Winnipeg. She let me know later, and of her decision to move to Vancouver, refused financial help, went out to work again, taking no holidays except to visit us in northern BC, saving for when she could work no more, and earned more in 1983 at her last job, when she was seventy-nine, than she ever had before in her working life. I had helped her find that apartment that had become her home, more spacious than any in which she'd lived, which now she must leave, and was feeling a keen sense of loss, and vulnerability, hers, and a quickening awareness of my own. Immediately after writing my last exam, I stopped to buy a paper, found an apartment just listed, with much the same layout as what she'd had, which I thought would make it easier for her to become accustomed to it, and it was within easy walking distance for her to shop. It had a balcony, which she had never had, a kind of raised patio overlooking blooming bushes of Solomon's seal and rhododendron crowding up to what would be her bedroom window, which overlooked a lane, a row of cherry trees, which I hoped would screen a self-serve gas station beyond them. It was even closer to where I was living and about the same rent. She hesitated, seemed disappointed. Was I was talking her into signing the rental agreement? I felt heavy of heart. When it came time for her to sign the deposit cheque, I watched her hand hover for a moment, then sign her name. Her hand hovered again, then set the pen down with an embarrassed smile, her eyes cast down, and I realized she was unable to complete the rest of the cheque. Dismay, the drowning depths of something primal in me, as I picked up the pen, stab of a child's terror, her child again, hugging her around the knees. She is looking down, laughing, holding her child and telling her she is growing so big, too big to pick up anymore, the child asking why she has to go to work, why can't she stay home? She is telling her child, "You aren't enough to stay home for." Always honest—*this* too honest for a child? A moment's pause while I composed myself, feeling the ache now, for her, the vulnerability in her embarrassment, and felt a child's fear in myself as I wrote the rest of the cheque for her, her inability to do so reverberating, shifting ground between us.

Concerned about the distress the move would cause Jean, I helped her pack, and my daughter and son-in-law moved everything to her new apartment while I took her for breakfast at a little neighbourhood restaurant. In my enthusiasm for her new patio/balcony, I bought a long cedar planter to set on the balcony's ledge. It took my daughter to observe and point out to me that Jean didn't like it. We removed it and bought some small plastic planters Jean picked out herself. It would be the beginning of many lessons to come—my learning curve would prove very steep. Jean never did take to her new apartment. Never seemed to feel at home here. Although she appeared to like the patio, where she sat in the summer and could see the blue of the north shore mountains through the trees. She did not forget to water the plants we bought together, the geraniums, carnations, roses and petunias, the pansies and zinnias, good prairie flowers; she never stopped watering them. They struggled, drowning, transformed to thick stalks, rampant green, bushy, gone wild, like the geranium that grew like a tree, searching for the light, years ago in our rooms on Osborne Street. But I overwater plants too.

Perhaps with intimations of a coming loss, I began to sense that Jean's life, its wholeness, who she really was, had escaped from a lifetime's experience of and with her that I had constructed from memories of a child, an adolescent, and a distant adult's perspective. What had given these memories, the heart of them, their shape, the way this child saw her own world and therefore that of her mother? Our circumstances, when I was a child, made her appear solitary to me, her friendships work-related, co-workers of whom she only occasionally spoke. I did not often see Jean display her emotions, express her feelings, or affection. An exception was the day she came home from work, ecstatic, because she'd finally come up on the agency list for an apartment in a building newly built after the war, surrounded in trees and overlooking the Assiniboine River. We could leave our rooms on Osborne Street. No matter the floods had come and we had to move out again, temporarily, a week after we had moved in. I don't think I had ever seen Jean visibly joyful. It was startling. I would be starting high school that fall. In adolescence I didn't pay much attention when she played bridge with neighbours in our new apartment building, away now from Osborne Street and rooms with no running water.

A few people came to our home once we lived there. I do remember babysitting for an office friend of Jean's, and some dinners to which Jean and I were invited. During the 1950 Winnipeg flood, when we had to evacuate our apartment, we went separate ways, Jean with an office friend and I first with one school friend, then another, for the two months or so before we could live in our home again. Other memories again began to drift up to consciousness, of people either Jean sought out, or who sought us out, after my father died ... some Christmas dinners with other families, one in rooms like ours on Osborne Street— their laundry hanging, strung across a steamy kitchen, as Christmas dinner cooked, and we shared it with a family of six, four almost grown sons and daughters, their mother working at Eaton's, their father, like mine, involved in education. They lived together in those four rooms above a second-hand bookstore. Another friend of my father's took me to baseball games for a time, sharing his love of the game with me.

Jean, independent, honest, hardworking, always surprised me with reams of poetry she could recite from memory. As the ground had begun shifting so immensely from under a lifetime of my perceptions of her, I saw that what I once thought of as her aloofness was really a deeply learned restraint, began to remember that neighbours who had any contact with her seemed to really like her and counted her as a friend. Friends from different times in my life also got along well with her, or liked her when they met her, often to my chagrin as a young adult and later, as I carried that lingering angst that her restraint had only to do with me, a reflection of her disapproval, her disappointment in who I was. In the years when we exchanged letters, Jean signed hers "Mother," or perhaps even "Mom." On a birthday card, when I was around fifty, she added the word "love." Why then, I didn't know. It was not a word Jean threw about lightly. I recently discovered the following note from me to Jean, written on the back of a postcard I sent to her from camp one summer, when I was fourteen or fifteen. The postcard had been stuck face up in a photo album for many years, the note forgotten: *Dear Mom, Sorry I haven't written you more often, but these cards are 15 cents for 2 without stamps. I had some swell kids in my patrol. They came third in the contests. I think you had better send a sheet and a pillow case if* ("if" is underlined several times) *I am staying down a third week. I haven't been sick and I'm having a terrific time. Please write if you feel like it, love Frances xxoo* There was four cents due on the postcard. I was struck by my ease with my mother that I expressed there, that I seemed to have forgotten.

As I wrote, a memory came, then another, and I was back again in that small hamlet where my life began, sitting under the dining-room table. Above me the talk goes on and on, people in for dinner, my mother, father, there. I have with me a little egg cup full of cooked fresh green peas from our garden. A smell of roast lamb dinner, possibly a mince pie, the light dim, turning tablecloth lacework where it hangs down over the edge of the table a soft pale shade of tea ... then my mother sitting at a desk, perhaps a sewing table by the window in the dining room, near the door to the basement, a root cellar, very scary place full of root and earth smells and no light. I am very small, this is my earliest memory. I have my father's tools, his hammer, and I am smashing the little window to the root cellar, hidden down behind green weeds growing up around it. The glass is falling into the weeds in shiny pieces. I don't remember my father and mother saying anything to me about it. My mother was learning shorthand to work as a secretary—she never did get her typing up to speed and bookkeeping is what she eventually did for a living, when we left for Winnipeg. While she works I am in the kitchen with a large patient farm dog who comes by from time to time, I think my mother feeds him, after once bandaging his injured paw ... I am putting curlers in his shaggy fur and rolling whatever I can find in kitchen cupboards to spread on his back, oatmeal flakes, raisins. She did not rebuke me for this. There were dresses she made for me, a green one in some kind of soft fluffy material, with flowers, and winter suppers in the kitchen with sliced raw onions soaked in vinegar on top of mashed potatoes and warm winter puddings. She was a good cook. Saturday funny papers came off the train from Winnipeg and echoes, stones and voices colliding, from the curling rink across the road. The world was white and silent through an eye hole melted in window frost by my small hand, relieved only by the jingle of the horse's bells out there, as they dragged sledges carrying water over the snow, and brought children to school. The wind beyond the reaches of my child's mind carried on it the wail of a train across a winter plate of frozen snow, cracking time from space, splitting my cocoon open to outer space spiralling away from me I knew not where.

Jean's life during the span of time, from when I left home to now, 1989, I knew only by its contours, her visits to us, to our wedding, to visit her grandchildren. No "extravagances." In her early sixties,

Jean hitched a ride on the small airline she worked for, to Ottawa, then bused to Toronto to visit our family, and her grandchildren. There were two by then. She went on to New York, again by bus, and flew from there to Britain, sleeping on the trains as she travelled to Scotland and her parents' birthplaces, completely exhausted when she returned. Somewhere in those years she had worked as a volunteer on the election campaign for Pierre Trudeau. In the several years after she no longer went out to work, I know she did not see herself as old, and once indicated to me that "sitting on park benches" was not something she liked to do. She said she found seniors' groups in her area "clique-ish," preferring to spend her time in other ways, on very little money. Her daily walking increased once she missed the routine and rhythm of going out to work. There were a few neighbours with whom she had contact, particularly once she no longer had a job to go to, but the eviction disrupted further connection. One neighbour told me how much she would miss Jean once the eviction took place. There were no holiday trips, other than to visit us. She was impelled, like many who lived through those years of the Great Depression, the so-called dirty thirties, to save themselves from poverty and despair, or the fear of it, if they could.

Wild Heart

Over the summer of 1989, Jean was coming to some kind of terms with her new apartment. I was trying to write, and feeling the weight of Jean, myself, the prospect and possibility of needing to become a full-time daughter again, or perhaps for the first time. I had also begun remembering my dreams, something I had not done since childhood. They were confusing and seemed to be about death—no colour, either dark or light, occasionally sepia. Sam had taught me to walk, and through walking to discover how meditative, almost trance-like, rhythmic movement could be, releasing knots in the heart and mind. Over the summer we spent much time along the ocean beaches and through forest trails out by the university, where, once classes resumed, we would go again, on the way to, and returning from my courses, which I scheduled so Sam would not be left alone at home or in the car for too long at a time. She had become my constant companion.

At water's edge, a smell of iodine, sulphur, and iron along the tide line, ocean tumbling, rolling and breaking over exposed rocks, flinging its voice across a lip of shore where slatey blue herons stood fishing in shallows, eyeing us, wet streaming from tousled feathers, seeming oddly dishevelled, caught at play. White gulls nestled among red kelp, barnacled rocks, scissoring dead fish, the light angling down, vibrating, turning rock to flesh. Rock a piled-up hardness of broken magma, softness hardening to it. What of the soft underbelly of the child? What does it mean to cling, barnacle to rock, to survive and breathe, in and out of water, on shores of heart space?

Labour Day weekend, just before my return to classes, I woke up feeling the approach of another migraine growling around the edges of consciousness, waiting to take over, but then a delicate green morning enfolded a call of gulls diving deep, soaring high. I remembered the gulls crying and circling above my head in a field far from water. Gulls coating the rises and furrows of plowed fields, the sound of them high and circling over stubble fields that slid away, fooling the eye into an illusion of smoothness, uniformity; up close, they are unsmooth and ragged. Fields of kinship. My clock alarm went off—6:00 a.m. Later, walking with a friend in green-dappled forest light, there were more feelings of illness, the returning migraine blurring and intensifying my senses, headache and nausea, disorientation, vague spacey-ness. But also a kind of physiological euphoria, the walk alive with possibilities, light caught on dewy leaves and spider webs gave a sense of possibilities, of tiny wings, presences. We shared our dreams; mine had begun to occur almost as regularly as sleep. Along the walk we found a nest of baby garter snakes sliding out of a hole in the ground, seven of them, the last little one paused, uplifted face watchful, hopeful, vulnerable, feeling no threat from us, moving ahead like wind in the grass, leaving me with a memory of the friendly faces of helicopter fish behind glass, when this friend and I visited the aquarium over the summer, and the belugas there, their gift of themselves, of the benign, life's benevolence that is by no means simple. I needed this reassurance. By afternoon the headache was back, workmen downstairs were replacing carpet tiles, a toxic smell of glue wafted up through the heating vents. I took some work to the water. A cold wind turned a blue ink sea to rough milk green, clouds shaped an anvil over the city. The wind began to clear my head, rent and shredded the clouds until they fell apart across the sky and turned to disappearing smoke. Sam restless as always. For a retriever she had an odd fear of water, would not go in, until a week before she died, when she waded in up to her shoulders and stood there. Putting her toe in, perhaps, trying it out before she left? Jean had a fear of water too, had never learned to swim, had trouble putting her face into water. She made sure I took lessons.

Back at university for a second part-time term, I felt a need to move beyond my fear of what I didn't know lay ahead. A kind of homesickness had struck as a painful recognition of changing moments of place, landscape, and of relationship, the natural world the only continuous relationship available. The child there, without warning, in those shifting moments drawing down like wings of birds. I dreamt my mother had died and I was told this by others after I had left her alone. I seemed to have hit a wall, which, I would later learn, over and over again, was that timeless child within, her fear, not Jean. Whatever Jean may have been experiencing now, as a result of her heart's fibrillation on the operating table, some sixteen months ago, whether since then her time, space, motion were becoming disjointed, leaving her stranded, perhaps losing her sense of who she was, she voiced no demands or fears, nor expressed to me what she may have been experiencing. I would never know whether she had been told by her doctors to expect the possibility that her memory, her orientation in time and space would be affected, or not. I was unaware myself, at this point, of the implications of that fibrillation event, but had begun to feel at some more unspoken, intuitive level, that Jean was reaching for me. I had begun to experience fear, panic, and anger, without knowing their source. Out for dinner with a friend, I realized it was October 17, the date of my father's death, forty-two years ago. As we talked, there was news of a 7.1 magnitude earthquake in California. A freeway overpass had collapsed. Emotional plates were shifting in me. I couldn't seem to find solid ground.

A month later, a sudden onset of chemical sensitivity to what seemed like everything in my environment, caused my body weight to drop precipitously; taking medical leave from the university for the remainder of the fall semester was the only option. Obviously my body wanted to shed something, but what? The doctor I saw identified it all as an allergy to grains, wheat in particular, suggested I avoid grains for up to a year. I wondered how long I could live on just lettuce, cucumber, and avocado, which was all I could tolerate just then without a reaction. The reactions were not pleasant, and included, along with the more common reactions related to food allergies, a sudden inability to remember my name, where I was going, and the ensuing panic this produced. Was I being prepared for what Jean was undergoing? I feared I was losing my ability to rationally think, know, and therefore be, found myself sitting at my computer, unable to write, and it seemed I was living in a Doris Lessing novel, the one on our course reading for that year, in which words and their meanings break down when there is a split in the self … an inundation of words that confused, meanings that slipped away, trying to match them with what was happening inside me, this unnamed place beckoning to me like an unmade bed I was about to fall into; caught between opposing forces of mental containment and heart chaos. A friend suggested seeing a counsellor; gave me the name of someone who, she said, was wise and compassionate. I resisted, perhaps afraid of what I might find out about myself. Then, without giving myself any reason, I called and made an appointment. This would begin the ongoing work-in-progress that life would continue to be, identifying those parts of me which seemed to have come loose and taken on a life of their own, naming them, like anger, fear, panic, sadness, regret, guilt, and tracking their source, to perhaps understand them better, come to terms with them.

The memories, the dreams had come for a reason; they were not just emotional baggage; confusion would continue playing its part. I found myself needing, not always willingly, to go back to the mother/ child relationship. Fear with no identified focus produced panic, an elemental need to run, escape. I found it spreading everywhere, my writing, studying for a degree, being on my own, being who I was, finding out who I was … responsibility, I can't do it, the panic was telling me. In what was perhaps Jean-like fashion, I realized, later, I did not tell my children any of this, other than the health issues, and some of my concerns about Jean. They knew I was seeing a counsellor. Not burdening them with added worries about me was, to some extent, also a rationalization—there was likely some shame, guilt, for not being able to handle whatever this was, and how it would affect my "mother" image, whatever that might be, to admit to "losing control." Christmas, my sons came back to Vancouver for the holidays. There is a photo taken in the living room of what had for me become home; in it Jean sits on the sofa with her two grandsons, my daughter and son-in-law are sitting on the floor with Sam, in front of a Christmas tree decorated with ornaments from many family Christmases ago. My children are laughing, and Jean is looking at Sam, and smiling a little self-consciously. The one strongest connection, anchor, in my life had always been my children. Perhaps they felt me leaning on them then, and at other times, as I was feeling Jean, in ways unspoken. Bonds between parent and child run deep and defy definition, or expectations.

Panicked and feeling like a scared child who had run away from home, or life as I'd known it, and didn't know what to do next, I began to understand how inaction fed fear, one in particular, that my life would disappear into Jean's. I would have to tell her of my need, not to be burdened to give what I couldn't. When I told Jean that I couldn't be the one she depended on for everything, it was with a pent-up anger that burst out of me and ranged freely. She listened, silent, then told me to get this "sickness out of my system if I must ... why go over what's past?" Jean's words, whatever she meant by them, were lost in the shock I was feeling, appalled by the intensity of anger that had, quite unexpectedly, burst out of me. The anger felt ancient, stored up. Jean told me then that she didn't want me to spend a lot of time with her, that she didn't need a lot of people or places to go. That she had always lived alone. She could take care of herself. I felt acutely a history of our absence from one another, and an unsettling mixture of relief and anxious guilt. Jean was eighty-seven. Had I abused my aging mother? I explained my medical leave from classes at UBC. Jean was concerned, supportive, sympathetic. "Take care of yourself," she said. She was interested and pleased when I told her, for the first time, of my writing. My realization was sharp that not only did I not really know this woman who was my mother, I had not been willing to know her, even though I thought otherwise, nor had I shared essential parts of my life with her. A sad realization, and a chink in the child's wall through which could be seen another way to live in this body, without the paralysis of silence.

I returned to classes later that winter, wrote all my postponed exams in the spring and planned to return the fall of 1990 to complete my arts degree. Exactly where I was in the school of fear remained to be seen. Applying for entrance into the master's program in creative writing at UBC began to seem possible. In June, I flew to Toronto to visit with my sons. There were side trips to Ottawa by train for a weekend and to Niagara-on-the-Lake for the Shaw Festival, organized by each of them. I was touched by their thoughtfulness and the time they took to be with me. We were all adjusting to changing realities in our lives. A dream, before returning to Vancouver, was labyrinth-like and repetitive ... I am a child, wandering streets that seem to be in Winnipeg, somewhere north of Portage Avenue, and heading what feels like south, roaming streets, taking a streetcar, nowhere in particular that I can recognize. Then there is a woman, who seems to be a writer, xeroxing a short story. A child begins running, looking backwards over her shoulder, and falling.

I had begun taking tai chi later in the summer and found during the course that I was losing my balance. The instructor told me it was a good sign, things were shifting, that balance was about our every movement flowing into another, bringing ease and flexibility to body, mind, and spirit. So for the moment, I guessed, my various movements would be falling and bumping into one another, without much decorum.

The Labour Day weekend had arrived, and with it the high-pitched mosquito-like whine of the Indy 500 cars racing around Vancouver's downtown streets. I was preparing to return to classes the following week. Jean called to say she was feeling unwell. By the time I arrived and had started some breakfast for her, she had collapsed onto the floor of her bedroom. I couldn't lift her. She wasn't responding. The paramedic I spoke with, a woman, said they would turn off the siren as they approached Jean's home. When they arrived, they were gentle, quiet, conversational, and I blessed them for their thoughtfulness. She was taken by ambulance to a hospital emergency ward. We arrived as several injured had also arrived, from an accident at the Indy 500, and were being treated; one young man had been killed. Eventually Jean was examined, found to be bleeding internally and was given transfusions. Jean would also be given ranitidine for the five days she remained in hospital. Later, I would learn that this is the same family of drug as the cimetidine she was given in 1988 prior to her mastectomy. In the aging this drug is known to be associated with an increased risk for confusional states and depression. Agitation and hallucinations have been reported, as well as heart arrhythmias, premature ventricular beats and loss of the rhythmic contractions of the chambers of the heart to form a pulse.

At 6:45, the morning after Jean was admitted to hospital, prior to undergoing an endoscopy procedure, her medical records indicated she was confused, had gotten out of bed, removed her IV and blood transfusion line, described in nursing notes as: *pt. confused, disoriented to person, place, time, inappropriate speech.* Her IV and blood transfusions were restarted. She was seen by a gastroenterologist, who recorded: *chronic atrial fibrillation ... GradeIII/VI systolic murmur at the left sternal border radiating to the apex....* He performed an

upper gastrointestinal tract endoscopy procedure to assess the source
of the bleeding. For this Jean received 5 mg of intravenous diazepam
(a benzodiazapine) for sedation. Jean was already on ranitidine, which
increases the effects of diazepam, such as central nervous system
sedation, confusion, disorientation, and short-term memory loss.
The endoscopy indicated the source of bleeding to be likely from a
duodenal lesion and that Jean also had gastric irritation, likely due, it
was thought, to the possibility she may have been taking Aspirin before
going to bed, for headache pain. I later found a bottle of sleeping pills
in her linen closet, prescribed by her then GP. It did not look as though
any had been taken. Jean's hospital admission records, supplied by this
GP, at this point, in 1990, indicated: *chronic atrial fibrillation.* He told
me a little later that he had to "fight with her to get her to take her
digoxin." I wondered if Jean was attempting to tell him she felt the
dosage of digoxin was affecting her negatively? During this current
hospitalization, Jean's daily dosage of digoxin was reduced to 0.0625
mg from the level of 0.25 mg she'd been prescribed and had been
maintained by her GP since she left hospital after her mastectomy in
1988. Had this level overdosed her into the toxic range, the digoxin
itself causing arrhythmia and related damage, from 1988 to1990? Now
her electrocardiogram indicated atrial fibrillation. On the fourth day of
this hospital stay, an echocardiogram was done and indicated: *severe
left ventricular hypertrophy and mitral and tricuspid regurgitation.* It
had been two years since her heart went into atrial fibrillation under
inhalant anaesthesia for mastectomy, for which, her records stated, *no
reason was found.* Succeeding cardiovascular exams would appear in
her records that indicated a damage, which earlier records demonstrated
was not seen prior to that event. This information was not available
to me at that time. Distressing to find these omission and oversights
later, as I searched her hospital records, having obtained them after
her death, under freedom of information legislation. Also later, would
I learn that medical literature identifies toxic blood levels of digoxin
variously as: above 1.4nmol/L., above 1.6, and above 2.0. The dosage
of digoxin administered to Jean in hospital in 1990 remained at .0625
mg for her discharge home. At some point much later, under the care
of the same GP, her records indicated the blood level of digoxin, was at
1.8nmol/L.

September 5, while she was still in hospital, Jean's GP wrote in
her records: *Medically stable but very confused and disoriented,*

ruminating about losing her purse somewhere, fairly oriented to person and time but confused re place and who I was exactly, but knew she was "somewhere" and that I "always look after her." He made no connection in the record to the drugs being administered to her and their physiologically toxic effects, nor the stress she had undergone generally, and suggested a CT scan might be of use. Nursing notes the same day indicate: *pt. somewhat confused, disoriented to place, concentration fine.* September 6, Jean is described: *somewhat disoriented to place and time, recalls month and hospital and home address, eating well and caring for herself and anxious to go home "to my own environment where I know where everything is."* I recall a nurse telling me then that they "lost" Jean for a time and found her downstairs on the third floor "shopping for dresses at Eaton's." I spoke with the nurse and the resident doctors about effects of the particular medications she was on, particularly the ranitidine and misoprostol, prescribed for her in relation to the emergency GI bleed she had experienced. Risks associated with misoprostol include neuropathy. In older people, over sixty years, adverse effects can occur from what is considered a standard dose. After my comments to the nurse and residents, both ranitidine and misoprostol were stopped, replaced with sucralfate. Jean was discharged with a prescription for this, and digoxin at the reduced level of .0625 mg. For the first few days Jean was home again, I stayed overnight. She seemed to me to be noticeably disoriented, confused. When a pharmacy delivered her medications to her door in a bubble pack, meant to keep track of each day's pills, on a weekly basis, Jean didn't appear to know what they were, or who sent them. I don't know if this bubble pack was ever discussed with Jean. She was embarrassed, angry, as I tried to explain the reason for them being sent to her this way, that they had been ordered for her by her doctor. There was shiny aluminum backing in each bubble. She didn't seem able to find the little white digoxin pills, or the large whites sulcrafates. Additional iron sulphate pills in the pack added to the confusion. I would find the tiny white digoxin pills on the floor under her table, sometimes in the garbage. When the pharmacists refused to make any changes, I picked up her bubble packs myself and taped over all the confusing times and dates printed on them, which seemed to help.

Jean's legs had always been slender, with no ankle swelling, but in hospital they had swelled enormously, and remained so now she was home. I grew alarmed at the size of them and urged her doctor to visit her at her home, which he did, prescribing another pill for the bubble pack, a diuretic. He complained about her "non-compliance," was unwilling to discuss the possibility of adverse effects from all these medications. This doctor's solution was to "get her into a nursing home." He ordered a CT scan to be done at the same time as a follow-up endoscopy scheduled to confirm there was no further duodenal bleeding. The CT scan indicated nothing abnormal. After having the scan, Jean was upset. She apparently had asked what it was for and was told by a nurse it was " to see if your brain is okay." After a few weeks, I was finally able to get this doctor to stop all the medications, except digoxin. He seemed stressed and irritated by my mother. And me. Jean was noticeably better once these drugs were stopped, had no further swelling of her legs, and we moved, then, through an interlude in which Jean seemed to regain some equilibrium.

Memory Dissolving Time

Thanksgiving weekend, 1990, I was on Saltspring Island. Crows were clicking in arbutus trees twisting and winding their way up over shale and water, their red berries staining shale. The crows flew at my head. Shale split into slippery layers where the tide had been, like memory dissolving time, space, breathing.

The ferry brought me home again to my telephone's hungry red eye, blinking, blinking, message tape full of Jean's sobs, "what's happening to me, someone out there please help me, this is Jean…. (she gave her full name as it had been before her marriage to my father and I thought, with a pang, that this week was the anniversary, again, of his death, Jean's loss of him). I am looking for Fran Muir, she will know who I am…." Something exposed, from beneath that seamed absence of breast, coming out of hiding; a wild, irregular beat calling Jean to go missing, along with her breast, from time and space. A rain of small clots, pooling around her heart, flung into her brain where they lodge, blocking her navigational aids, leaving her confused, anxious, until these constellations dissolve. Her universe contracts, then expands, and she can again tell her keys from her bus pass and her money. How to keep it under control?

Jean was eighty-seven and struggling monumentally to keep her independence, her privacy, and to cope with this random disorientation that had begun coming without warning and went the same way. I was attending a fuller schedule of classes during the day, teaching a writing course at night, taking care of an aging Sam, and dropping by to check on Jean. Her need for independence and making her own choices was not only strong, but, I believed, a right that needed to be respected. I was also navigating menopause, which, for me, was increasing rather than reducing the migraines I, from time to time, had experienced for the greater part of my life. These were becoming more frequent and more debilitating. I was unsure what to do for Jean. Her need for independence and making her own choices was not only strong, but, I believed, a right that needed to be respected. Arranging for homemaking service to help maintain her in her home seemed a way for both of us to go on.

My daughter and son in law would soon be leaving for a year in West Africa. During November, my daughter and I spent several days at a cabin by the ocean, along the southwest coast of Vancouver Island. When my birthday came up, also in November, she had invited me out to a film, and after we were on our way, through some means that seemed reasonable at the time, returned us to my place, where a surprise birthday awaited. She had garnered names and phone numbers from my address book and assembled everyone she could contact. I was overwhelmed, to say the least. There was a beautiful bouquet of flowers, a cake, and my son-in-law had manned the oven to produce various warm edibles. There had always been family "surprises" at Mother's Day, and so on, but I'd never had a surprise party and was unused to the attention. My daughter had done such a lovely and loving thing. I found myself overcome with a strange melancholy I couldn't shake.

Valentine's Day, 1991—Love is an awkward, delicate, inappropriate child with a grip that won't let go, I wrote in my journal, and ... *the timeless child ...? Who got left back there, where, when? Sam, my dog, is sick, costing a lot of money I don't have, or energy for all of this.* There were dreams of Sam going missing, searching for her in landscapes unfamiliar, yet not. We went out for a usual walk, Sam and I, a smell of wetness in morning air, city's hum and winter birds in wakening trees, found a dying pigeon on the curb under the boulevard maple trees' bare limbs laced against the sky; their roots fractured the sidewalk cement, twisted and ran, broken free of earth and grass. Sam had begun to pant and slouch.

A representative from the area health unit came to do a preliminary assessment of Jean's need for homemaker services. To Jean, it seemed that strangers were inviting themselves into her apartment, looking into her fridge and cupboards, asking personal questions that were none of their business, and telling her daughter, not her, as though she wasn't there, that she should not live in her own home anymore. It was strongly recommended to me that Jean be referred to an in-hospital geriatric assessment program, and also that I place her name on a waiting list for an intermediate care facility. Jean's frustration, anger, and resistance to losing control of her independent life and privacy seemed to me a reasonable response to her situation, what anyone would feel. But I began to search out various government-subsidized care facilities from a list provided by the health unit, to begin to familiarize myself with what was out there, and to keep future options open.

By April 1991, Jean had been assessed as qualifying for homemaker help. I was again urged to bring Jean to the geriatric assessment unit and was told that this assessment would be required before Jean would be accepted by a care facility subsidized by the government. I was feeling very cautious about interfering with the dignity of Jean's independence and sensed that what could be closing in on her basic desire, her human need, for personal autonomy, was a bureaucracy without the capacity to accommodate, dignify, or respect human personality and choice. Already, I had witnessed the system making limiting assumptions about Jean, based on minimal contact with her.

April as well, when Jean married my father, in 1931. Spring, when she took me on a train to Winnipeg, away from winter's frozen water pump, chimney fires, poplar logs too green to burn, the outhouse the boys in my father's class overturned every Hallowe'en, as I sat on his knee in the dark on our verandah and he told me it was just for fun, they didn't mean any harm by it. Away from lace tablecloths and people in for dinner, to a street, a city energized by war, where streetcars shook our building as they passed, rounded the bend, and disappeared.

April 1991, Jean was also assessed as entitled to attend a Friendship Centre for Seniors funded by the provincial government. A bus would pick her up. At first Jean seemed to like it, told me she'd had a good time, "Scottish people there and singing." A few days later she called to say she was "not feeling well, can't seem to do what I want to." I came over to make her dinner and prepare some food ahead. She seemed appreciative, in good spirits, accepted all my help. I noticed her file folder out on the table, her bank books and cheques out. She was using her cheques to make notes to herself. When I accompanied Jean to the Friendship Centre they would tell me she "doesn't join in, or converse, just watches, doesn't think she's old or needs the activities here," that she "needs to be brought back to reality...." which seemed to be about the kind of behaviour they expected and needed within the framework of their way of organizing things, and what was assumed when individuals didn't fit their program. When Jean and I sat down for lunch at the Friendship Centre, there was a quiet gentleman at the end of the table, who was from Manitoba. He and my mother seemed to be enjoying each other's company, but their conversation, and everyone else's, was continually interrupted by a slender, bright-eyed woman who kept repeating, "My sister was tops in school in the city in the province in the country, did you know her? tops in everything—perfect, I wasn't." We ate more or less in silence as she searched for what, who, got lost on the way to there. If someone had put their arms around her, become her older sister, and told her she was perfect too, and loved, as many times as she needed, would it have made a difference, could she have been comforted to let it go?

In the days following, Jean told me she could remember her childhood exactly, everything about it, better than things now. She spoke of Sam the horse taking water from the well to the garden, taking her to school across the snow-filled fields, waiting there to take her home again. Her Sam and my Sam, a coincidence of names; hoofbeats, heartbeats. After Jean had gone out for groceries, she called me to say she "had to lie down, it was just a light bag, can't do what I want." Getting herself out to the Friendship Centre, or to the store, or having the homemakers in, keeping herself together, was it all just too much? Not sure she'll go to the Friendship Centre anymore, angry at having so many appointments, dentist, doctor ... and too many things. She had put away, out of sight, her coffee maker, and the little one-cup filter cone I brought her; had everything stored away in drawers. She had also thrown out a lot of stuff, including most of her photos and her lease agreement for her apartment. A cry for space, her own rhythm.

By May, Jean seemed to have decided she would take a little help from the homemakers, who were coming by now, or attempting to do so, and was home most of the time when they arrived. She called me, very upset, because they had told her they needed loonies for the washer and she didn't know what *loonies* were, loonies having recently replaced dollar bills, but once I explained she understood; *not* knowing was what upset her. I didn't see evidence that she was eating very much of the food that was prepared for her. When she thought she would like to shop for some clothes to wear to the Friendship Centre, I was heartened. We went downtown, but she lost interest quickly, wanted to have lunch. It was difficult to watch her hesitant moves to cut her meat and navigate her lunch. Jean had always been graceful in movement, elegant in dress. She pondered the cluster of grapes on her plate, fingering them self-consciously as if blind, until touch discovered how to part each of them from their stem. Still graceful, still elegant. Her apartment manager reported to me, when we met in the hallway, that Jean had told him "her daughter had left home." His eyes accused. Did Jean feel abandoned? Was she back when her daughter did leave her, on another train, east to Toronto? Was she afraid I would run from her again?

May 16, 1991, Jean began attending a hospital geriatric assessment unit on an outpatient basis. Her attendance required, I had been told, to provide Jean with further services in her home as well as facilitate her acceptance into what was referred to as an Intermediate Care Facility. I had already viewed a number of these government-subsidized facilities offering this care, in order to put Jean's name on a wait-list. It was a dismaying task, observing the range of institutional care. Some of it appalled, none comforted. There were too many absent faces, sad and silent eyes, too many overly loud voices calling into ears that might be neither deaf nor infantile. I eventually found one that was new, bright, the walls a light yellow. There were gardens, cats, a fireplace, piano, birds. What convinced me was the word *respect*, which was used frequently, the emphasis on respect for the residents and their choices. I placed Jean's name on the waiting list for this facility, wanting it not to come to this, knowing I had no idea how she would make this decision, if she must. I was told it would be a year or longer before space would be available, and was relieved. I requested a referral to the geriatric assessment unit, against my instincts to the contrary. The unit's reference to an "intake" interview left me concerned about what Jean would be exposed to there. When I called the hospital, initially, for information, the person I spoke with, a nurse, was my impression, although not from within the unit itself, warned me, "think carefully about this; once in, the system takes over." Surprised by her candour, and feeling a threat to Jean in those words, which would prove prophetic, I was still faced with the bureaucracy's requirement of this unit's assessment before Jean, or anyone else in such circumstances, would be allowed more homemaker service to make it possible to remain at home. There seemed to be no alternative. A naive, more detached part of me rationalized that perhaps the unit would provide some insight into what Jean was experiencing. I was remembering the tears in Jean's eyes, when I was impatient when she tried to help after I spilled a jar of pickled beets in her fridge, and I had felt abusive and self-justifying.

Intake

On May 16, 1991, Jean's initial interview, referred to as an "intake," began with a review of her general medical history, taken by a physician she'd never seen before. I sat to one side, watched and listened. When the physician began asking questions about Jean's family and where she was born, she asked him why he was asking such personal questions, telling him she came from a good family, her mother and father were from "good healthy Scottish stock." When he persisted, saying he needed the information, Jean told him it was none of his business, at which point he began to pat her arm as though she was a child. She shrank back in the chair and said "don't touch me." I had never seen Jean like this. It seemed completely out of character and obvious that something had deeply agitated her. Her childhood was unknown to me at this point, but the wrenching in my gut, seeing this unexpected reaction in Jean, this expression of what felt to me like a child's fear, resonated a knowing in me that seemed at that moment to have always been, of some shadow in Jean's life. The term *post-traumatic shock* did not come to mind then, but later I would begin to recognize its features and learn its roots. I was then asked by this physician to leave the room, as though nothing had happened, so that a complete physical exam could be done, which seemed to me to be inappropriate at this juncture of such a reaction from Jean, who would then be left alone with two strangers, the doctor and an accompanying nurse.

After this doctor's examination, Jean and I waited together in a large common area. "Everyone is free, can make their own decisions," Jean said. I wanted to say, that goes for me too, but instead said, children sometimes aren't. Jean seemed to recognize, acknowledge what I'd said, although I didn't know if she referred it to herself or me; perhaps both. Later, when there had been interviews for both of us, mine with a psychiatric social worker, a nurse in charge of the unit began discussing with me, in front of Jean, Jean's "ability to shop appropriately for her food." Jean became upset and told this nurse she didn't want her to be "bothering people, family members, and putting pressure on them." The nurse apologized and tried to touch Jean's arm. "Don't touch me," Jean said, again, and pulled away from her. There was pressure to have Jean admitted as an in-patient, that a more effective assessment could be made this way. I did not see how a good assessment could be made of her abilities to cope if she was suddenly plunged into unfamiliar surroundings, with strangers who seemed to be operating from a model of pathology. They reluctantly agreed to her coming in as an out-patient, the plan being two days a week for six weeks. It did not take very long before Jean refused to return. She also began refusing to let the homemakers do anything for her, to give them money to shop, to let me open up an account at the local supermarket so they could buy what she needed, and began going out when the homemakers were scheduled to come to her home. I didn't see, right away, that this was a reflection of the threat her exposure to this geriatric assessment unit had imposed on her, to her privacy, as well as destabilizing Jean's confidence and sense of herself; what fears it was raising in her regarding her independence, her right to freedom and dignity of choice and risk. I was, at the same time, beginning to feel my own life being overtaken by the unpredictability of Jean's growing needs.

A phone call from Jean wakened me early in the morning. The hospital unit had called her to be picked up. She had told them she would not be going, told me her toilet wouldn't work, and indeed when I got over there, that was so. I showed her the chain inside the tank she could have pulled up, to fix it temporarily. There was no food in her fridge. She didn't want me to leave, saying the only problem was that I was not calling and she was alone too much. It was only the second time in my memory that she had mentioned loneliness. I remembered her words again, when I left home for my first job in Toronto, as she scrubbed kitchen cupboards, saying only, "You *will* come back sometime...?" And my shock.

After Jean's refusal to attend the assessment unit I was called to what was referred to as an "emergency meeting with the team," which consisted of health care professionals, including physicians, nurses, an occupational therapist, psychiatric social worker, a psychiatrist. Some of these individuals were residents in training. Here, I was informed that Jean was "uncooperative," because, they indicated, she would walk away from various group activities, such as baking cookies (Jean quit baking cookies once my children became adults) and would not stay to be interviewed by a psychiatrist. The doctor who had interviewed and examined Jean at her "intake,"was staring quite intently at me and suddenly asked me, with what felt to me like suspicion, why I told him I had no other family nearby. Since that interview, one of my sons had unexpectedly arrived to take up residence in Vancouver and had accompanied me to this interview. I sensed this doctor had taken Jean's reaction to him to be an indication of my possible abuse of her. The unit's psychiatrist, who'd had no interview with Jean, then described her as "paranoid, possibly psychotic, hallucinatory..." The purpose of this meeting was to secure my agreement to Jean's committal to what was described to me as "a secure facility." Riverview, an institution for the mentally ill, was mentioned. I realized then that my mother, always in my memory private, her reserve appearing aloof, and so very independent, in her refusal to return to this unit had been fighting for her life. Surrounded by ten or so health care professionals, doctors doing their residencies in geriatrics and psychiatry, I could feel the system, focused on "control," covering its bureaucratic backside, closing in on Jean. And the need to walk very carefully. Their interpretation of Jean's so-called behaviour, and their perception that she required managing in a secure facility, i.e., a institution for the mentally ill, I found appallingly precipitous and lacking in respect for what capacity Jean had for making her own choices. They appeared to me to be ignoring the obvious, that Jean was out of her familiar surroundings when here in this unit, that she was a private person, likely not comfortable in this environment with strangers, nor with being objectified with condescending and controlling attitudes. To say nothing of being re-traumatized by persistently insensitive professional behaviour.

I described, at this meeting, the fibrillation Jean experienced during the mastectomy in 1988. And the difficulties she experienced after her GI bleed several months previous. For the first time, the term "multi-infarct dementia" was used, filling the uneasy silence of those doctors in 1988 who were so focused on presenting their successful breast removal surgery that "got it all" to Jean and me. But at this unit, what was referred to as their "diagnosis" became a label with preconceived notions and attitudes attached to it. Jean was seen as demented, and the overriding issue became control of what was seen as out of control, and referred to in terms of "manageability," but what Jean was coping with was impairment of her short-term memory.

Medical literature indicates: the more profound acute anoxia (complete loss of oxygen to body cells that accompanies anaesthesia accidents) can result in brain damage and multi-infarct dementia, which is associated with these small strokes, called lacunae, which can destroy enough brain tissue to impair function either initially or over time whenever and as the heartbeat becomes irregular. Jean's fibrillation began under anaesthesia. Two years after this event, and after her GI bleed in the fall of 1990 and her exposure to various drugs, there followed a period of noticeable and, for her, uncharacteristic disorientation and short-term memory lapses. A CT scan showed no indications of any organic brain disease, or any indication of abnormality. Since her fibrillation on the operating table in 1988, digoxin, had been prescribed on a daily basis. Toxic effects from this drug, such as producing heart arrhythmia, or mimicking dementia, can occur at levels very close to normal therapeutic doses, or even idiosyncratically at what is considered a normal therapeutic dosage. Whether the *normal therapeutic dose* was in fact toxic to Jean and causing her heart arrhythmia episodes, or other symptoms is a possibility never raised in Jean's medical records. Her blood level of digoxin, when admitted to hospital in September 1990 for the GI bleed, does not appear to have been taken. I could find nothing in Jean's records to indicate this was done at that time, or that digoxin toxicity was considered as a possible source of the atrial fibrillation observed on her admission However, as indicated, her daily dosage of 0.250 mg of digoxin, prescribed in 1988, and apparently maintained by her GP since then, was reduced to 0.0625 mg on her discharge from hospital in 1990. Was her blood checked regularly for digoxin levels? I could find no evidence of this.

At this point Jean was still under the care of the same GP. As I came into more contact with this physician in the following months, he referred, several times, to an "ongoing battle to get her to take her digoxin," describing Jean as "uncooperative, non-compliant," writing this in records that would provide a basis for ongoing attitudes within the health care system toward Jean. I found him to be arbitrary, and prone to a frustration that could be aggressive, and had the sense he could become annoyed and badger her. The dosage of digoxin he was prescribing appeared not only to have been reduced by hospital medical staff in September 1990, when she was admitted to hospital for her GI bleed, but again, on entrance to this geriatric assessment unit, when the dosage under his care had again risen to 0.250 mg. This unit discharged Jean with a dosage halved. Other than standard blood tests and examinations, there was no record I could find of any digoxin blood levels having been checked for Jean during her brief time at this unit, after which the unit gave what they termed a discharge diagnosis as: *Chronic Organic Brain Syndrome, Senile Dementia, Multi-infarct but possible Alzheimer's component suspected as well.... Atrial fibrillation presumed due to atherosclerotic heart disease....* but on what basis? A psychiatric social worker on the team wrote in this report that Jean had "classic symptoms of dementia" which were then described as "a loss of inhibitions, split of personality, covering up of difficulties and inability to learn new things." I was concerned how this professional went about plugging Jean into this model, and the ease with which normal anger and frustration were deemed to be a "pathological loss of inhibitions." As for any "inability to learn new things," wasn't Jean coping with major events, the interruption of her short-term memory (which I believe should be distinguished from dementia as popularly defined as "losing one's mind, cognition," and certainly as defined by this psychiatric social worker) and her ability to orient herself in time and space? She was constantly learning how to cope. Jean never left her stove on. She threw out fresh food, rather than risk having left it too long. My sense was that when she couldn't remember and became confused, fear would panic her, which then made it difficult for her to focus and recognize what was what. Anyone who has endured a panic attack will know what this disorientation is like. Anxiety is also a natural coping skill.

These subjective, opinionated, and biased judgements about her mental and emotional state exposed Jean to labelling that became a danger to her. Under these circumstances it is possible for any one of us to be categorized as abnormal. I only become aware later, as I explored Jean's records, of how, in interviews with various individuals within the system, such as this psychiatric social worker, anything I may have said in response to questions regarding the history of our ongoing parent/child relationship would be pathologized in her records. What mother/daughter relationship isn't conflicted, complex? The ground was, and is still shifting under my assumptions of who she was, who I was then, and am now. At this time much of what I knew of Jean, as her daughter, her as my mother, and Jean herself, if it is possible to see your mother separately from her being your mother, was inarticulate, due to the nature of our relationship, who each of us were, and in part due as well to the stress I was under at that time to navigate our lives, our journey of shifting perspective in shifting circumstances, and learning to adapt to finding new ways of seeing both problem and solution.

Jean's experience with this unit greatly agitated her and did nothing to engender her confidence in her ability to cope. It should have been otherwise. Whatever they were saying to her, communicating to her by their attitudes in the few weeks she attended sessions before refusing to continue, seemed rather to erode her confidence and heighten her fears of losing control of her life and her basic right to all the choices she was capable of making. In the weeks immediately following, her phone calls became frequent, calling out for some reassurance, some navigational aid. Her clock radio had "blown up, two men came in to take it away, she couldn't tell time." Apparently her alarm came on during the night with a very loud buzz while she was sleeping. She ran out onto her patio or into the hallway calling "somebody help me." Someone, I assume the building manager must have come in and taped the alarm switch so she couldn't turn it on again.

By now Jean had been assessed as needing home assistance most days, but, in the wake of her experience at the hospital geriatric assessment unit, her resistance to homemakers who came intensified erratically. Their taping of a schedule of their visits on her fridge did not help, nor did the stream of different faces who appeared at her door. "I don't want strangers handling my food, they don't wash their hands, I don't need anyone to shop." When, finally, a primary homemaker was assigned, a battle of wills ensued. The individual would call me with a report on Jean. She seemed to have developed an adversarial situation with Jean, cooking food Jean didn't like, because it would be good for her, and rearranged Jean's cupboards, telling me that Jean put tea towels in the bathroom and bathroom towels in her kitchen. It made some sense to me when, finally, Jean refused to go shopping with this person and wouldn't give her any money to buy groceries, wouldn't let her near the kitchen. This homemaker quit, and I found myself shopping in between classes and preparing food, bringing it over. If she didn't remember where the food in her fridge came from, or when, she put it in the garbage; she would eat peaches steadily for a few days, or cheese, or tinned salmon, using things up, throwing them out before they went bad. During this time of agitation, Jean called me several times in the early morning to ask what I was "doing to her," that she'd "never forgive me," didn't "know what's happened," and left me her address, saying, "please call, hello, who is this?" When I explained why the homemaker quit and how difficult it might be for her to stay on her own, she said it would "kill her to move and that she didn't do anything to anybody." She wanted me to "vouch for her and believe her and not take their part."

A new primary homemaker, calmer, arrived on the scene. A Scandinavian woman who was gentle, loving, compassionate, and soft-spoken, who let me know I could call her any time and that she would call me, if there were concerns. Jean's cries for help had escalated with her agitation. Afraid she "has no money, can't get on a bus, doesn't have her keys, can't leave her apartment, afraid she will get lost, can't get to the bank, can't get any money to live or eat," saying she needed me "to come over and explain this to her, how it works. Is it the same as it always was?" If she "just does what she always does will it be alright?" Each time I returned home, her voice would be there on the answering machine, "Please call ... please help me ... please call ... it's very urgent." She called her apartment manager and told him she had no food, no money, no keys, and "Fran is gone." I found her emptying her purse, putting things away in drawers, then looking for them and taking them out again, unable, it seemed, to see what she was looking at, the money, the wallet, keys, bus pass were right there, confused then about what she was looking for. Names didn't seem to link with what she saw. Is this why there were so few clothes left in her closets, and hardly any photos from the steamer trunk, which had also disappeared? In concert with all this, my stomach lurched, dropped like a stone, my heart hid in fear. This was Mother. I was still waiting for everything, all that I felt had gone missing between us, not realizing, then, that it was already unfolding, and would, in its own way. For several more days the calls came intermittently on my answering machine, midnight, 6:00 a.m., every other hour for a day. She was angry, upset, crying, swearing. I had never heard Jean swear, or seen her cry, and it inexplicably, at that moment, stilled my own anger, which had also been escalating to cover fear, of helplessness, hers and mine. Then she suddenly called and said, "I'm back to normal. I know there's money in the bank. I'm okay, I went out and got some. But someone left a loaf of bread on my counter—some people come in here." She asked if my mother could come and visit her. I discovered she'd been taking several hundred dollars out of her account at one time, her way of taking control. I returned the money to her account, filed a note with her bank to call me if she took out any large sums of money. They were quite cooperative, but explained they couldn't monitor this to any great extent. I discussed with Jean, then, the need to make her accounts joint with me so that I could pay her bills and look after her money. She appeared to understand, her anxiety about money always there, but she seemed, at this point, to have regained her understanding that her money was safe, that I would take care of it, and that she could get it if she needed it.

Through Jean's episodes of panic and anxiety, confusion, interruptions of memory, of orientation, I began to learn I could talk her through them until she returned to calmness and seemed to be back to coping. Anxiety about not remembering was what appeared to cause her the greater confusion and panic. Reassurance, patient, and sometimes not-so-patient repetition (which always, in retrospect, causes sorrow in me) on my part allowed Jean time to struggle, monumentally, I believe, to come to terms with these episodes. She would later explain to me that she "can see everything but just can't find the words." I came to believe that she was trying to communicate with me as best she could, and in alternate ways, as her ability to call up words right away became difficult. And that she was often directly connected to what she carried in her, speaking a language that made perfect internal sense, such as asking me if my mother could come and visit her, which seemed also to be about her childhood friends. She asked if there was a man in her apartment, did a man come, did I have a man with me, did I have a brother? She had ten brothers, none of them living then.

I may have been named after a brother, Frank, who died before I was born. Awareness that comes when words are lost, that knowing we have as children, its directness, paying attention to what is there, is felt, without labels, moved between us.

What I began to see was a woman struggling heroically to come to terms with her life, whose desire was to be independent and care for herself, to make her own choices, with courage and great strength. She knew something was wrong. I saw dignity in her anger, rationality in her anxiety, her history in her fears. I saw Medea. She let me know that it took some time but she could finally figure things out if I would just hang in with her and go over it with her enough times. She did come to terms with things, recognized the necessity to do this, particularly when I expressed my own inability to cope, telling her I just couldn't handle it all. Then I saw something in her taking over, accepting, not willingly, or without anger, but as though protectively, of me, her child. Somewhere inside her she dealt with these massive changes even though the words were not there to express that process in logical terms.

During Jean's and my encounter with the geriatric assessment unit, I had informed them that Jean was already wait-listed for an intermediate care facility, that we would wait for space to come available and that I believed she had a right to make her own choice, and at this point it was not at all clear to me that she was not able to make that choice. Since Jean's refusal to return to the unit, and my indication to the unit that she would not be back for any more visits, I received two separate phone calls, one from the psychiatrist there, another from the head nurse of the unit, to tell me they thought my mother should "be hospitalized and put into care to keep her safe." They were, they said, "concerned that she is at risk." They urged me to reconsider. The psychiatrist said she was "very concerned Jean could be a danger to herself and others." Something in their comments and attitude definitely felt dangerous for Jean. Jean was again referred to as "unmanageable and needing a secure unit." I told them no, did not follow the advice I was given by this psychiatrist to "seek incompetency of Jean through a lawyer and obtain power of attorney," or to have them "certify her," take her away for "emergency placement in a secure facility." I was horrified by their intention. The psychiatrist's suggestion that a care facility of my choice might refuse to take her if she was "unmanageable" felt to me like a threat, pressure to be co-opted by them. The unit's head nurse then called me back, and I listened as she said, referring to Jean, "if she's unwilling we can certify her as incapable, incompetent, and send an ambulance to come and get her…" Mistaking my silence, she added, "You don't have to be there." I thought of their word, *intake*, of being caught in a machine, both Jean and I. What I did decide to do was negotiate for a psychiatric outreach team from the area health unit to do the assessment this unit was unable to do, for them to do this in Jean's home, in her familiar surroundings. This would take place some weeks later. In the meantime, both Jean and I were dealing with the aftermath of our experience with a unit that should have demonstrated, at the very least, more insight into Jean's situation.

Later, shortly after those phone calls I received from the unit, on a warm July night, I came to Jean's home to see if she would like to go for a drive. Shrinking away from me she flattened herself against the bedroom doorway, said, "Where are you taking me? I need to know where it is you are taking me." A drive, and some ice cream, I told her, stunned by the fearful reaction to me I saw in her. At this moment, after those phone calls I'd received from representatives of the unit, I was seriously concerned they, or even her GP, might have communicated to Jean some suggestion of a committal, threatening her already beleaguered sense of safety. I was dismayed that Jean might be seeing me as having betrayed her. "Oh," she said, immediately relaxing, looking pleased, surprised. This was new, this power to please her, and too heavy a measure of her vulnerability to bear. I would learn later, but had no idea at this point, what that unit would be circulating to various departments I would be continuing to deal with, and Jean's GP, regarding both of us.

Stars, Fish, and Gardens

We sat in the soft dusk with our ice cream, up on Jericho Hill, watched the lights twinkling like stars from across English Bay, and the freighters in the bay. "I can see it all," Jean said, her voice, her words glowed like fish in the darkness around us. "I can see it all," her hand reached into the air, "I just can't find the words," Tell me what you see, I said, wanting where I'd never been, inside the private life of the person who was my mother, wanting what both of us could be losing. Suddenly I was a child listening to stories she had never told me about her life, the farm where she grew up, the animals, cows running to water when they were kept in too long, the trees her father planted as a shelter from the wind, close up to the house, the heat further out, and all around on the prairie. Waiting up in a tree, twice as tall as her, for her family to come home from town, the mile-and-a-half walk to town and school, her frozen painful feet in winter, the snakes coming in from the fields sending her running into the house. Her ten brothers and herself, the youngest. Her mother, Jane, my grandmother, from Edinburgh, how hard her mother worked and never anything for herself ... the colours of the flowers around the house, the garden; tears

Jean and her mother, Jane.

running down Jean's cheeks, as from an underground stream. We were two children hidden in what shadows? *Tell me what you see* is how we would go on ... and I would tell her what I saw, for she did not seem to remember my childhood, until I told it to her, but this came later on our journey, breaking out into timeless spaciousness, into past silences, absences, the gaps between us, into mind's heart, heart's mind.

I thought of the young woman, Jean, I had seen in photos, the one I remembered as a child, who now was free floating in memory, perhaps coming to terms with, and finally expressing who she was, what she lost, whatever got left behind, had been silenced, and was being silenced again with attempts to render her "manageable." She was breaching that silence, expressing her anger, rage even, over attempts to treat her normality as "abnormal." Retrieval of some lost child a shared journey of remembrance, is this what Jean and I were on, each of us children together in the garden, her mother's garden, my mother's garden? What if I had let the geriatric assessment unit send their ambulance to take her away? How many others are taken?

"No money," she told me, that she worked to finish grade twelve, taught school (didn't mention her father's death, her return from university in Winnipeg to her penniless mother). "Terrible little towns," she said of those prairie places where she taught school, as drought and depression took hold of them. Where did you meet my father? "Who?" I asked her if she met my father, her husband, when she was teaching in Winnipeg. "Yes," she said. The rest went missing then, as her memory moved to "saving enough to go out west," to Vancouver in 1970, let go from her job at sixty-five, no pension, "moving while she still could," she told me then, asked if I'd ever done any travelling, told me I should travel once I'd finished university. Was she thinking of her daughter, me, or of herself and what she didn't get to do? When we returned to her home, she used her key to get into the apartment building and her own apartment without a problem.

By this summer of 1991, I had completed requirements for a BA in English literature and had been accepted into the master's program in creative writing, also at UBC. The program would begin in September. As Jean's fear had come in waves, fear of being alone, poor, of not being able to go out to get what she needed, of being taken away, and her confusion fed fear and panic in her, my own fear followed in tandem with hers. I had to survive, too, I was telling myself; will she sacrifice my life for her own survival, unaware she's doing it? But it was not

Jean doing this, it was her, our, circumstances. Yet, I could feel my own anger, frustration rise with each wave of her calls on my answering machine, accusations I was going to "put her away ..." What have I done with her money...? She needs me to come and "get everything straightened out. ... Fran, what's happening to me?" she would say, after the wave had subsided and before the next one hit, and we would talk. I explained again that her memory had been affected, and all these things she was worried about had been looked after, her money, her shopping, that I was close by and that homemakers would come to help her. As she seemed to recognize and accept this, she said, suddenly, "Oh my god, is this what's been happening?" Her immediate concern was "the bother to me" in what she had been doing and grief welled up in me in response; the ground under me shifted again. When I suggested to her, for the first time, that she could live where there was help for her at all times, she said quite clearly she wanted to stay where she was and "promises she will do better." Suddenly, calmness returned. Jean was very tired, but seemed to know what was happening, asked when the homemaker was coming, and recognized, or seemed to, that she could have her do some shopping and, for the first time, asked if the homemaker could do some cooking.

When the next wave hit, scattering time, location, words, I put labels on things. Jean took them off. When I came to fill her empty fridge, offered to cook some meals for her, she seemed upset by it, told me she didn't need it, called later saying she was "alone with no one to help her," and asked me if I "know where her daughter is," do I "know her address," she's "lost it." I returned with food, a roast, vegetables, fruit, an apple dumpling for desert. I came to make you supper, I told her. But Jean didn't want me to do this, said she "doesn't need this, just to talk, we never talk." We have never talked, I thought to myself, feeling anger rise, and wanted her to acknowledge her needs and their effect on me. Exasperated because if I didn't cook, there would be nothing for her to eat until the homemaker came again, and what if she didn't let them in, like last time, I told her, feeling my voice rise on my words, opening the fridge door for her to see its emptiness. Jean held her stomach and wouldn't look. I slammed the fridge door shut. "Sssh," she whispered at me, "sssh, they'll hear you." Who will? My voice louder than it should be, I grabbed the packages of food off the table, slammed them down on the kitchen counter. Jean looked as though she would have liked to shoo me away somewhere if she could. "Everyone," she said, her voice breaking on a whisper, "everyone will hear. I don't want them to hear how you are treating me." If only I knew then what later I would, I would have understood where this came from in Jean, the heartbreak of a child's learned shame. But all I saw then was my mother, her hands holding onto her belly, her last year's bleeding ulcer a weapon striking me in my own gut—it felt as though we shared the same one. How I'm treating you? This isn't working, I can't take care of you, I said. You need to find a place where they can do all this for you. My voice was still louder than I wanted it to be, and Jean was clutching at her stomach, telling me, "Don't talk to me like that, I'm old, I can't stand it. I didn't ask you to do this. I don't *want* you to do it." She grabbed at my arm, my hands, her hands unfamiliar on me, strong and delicate, wings of a bird against my skin, before she turned away, covering her face in them, shoulders heaving. No sound panicked me. I could hear my mother's voice as she turned from the telephone, "Daddy's dead" and the question there in her voice, "You'll be alright, won't you," that wasn't a question so much as the way things needed to be, and knowing then I'd have to be. In the goneness of him marked by no visible tears, the schoolmate who had told me I couldn't have loved my father because I came back to school too soon after he died, was only asking what it was like for a father to die. I could only answer her with silence.

I meant to take Jean's arm and lead her to a chair, but she pulled away with a cry, clenched her fists, came across the kitchen, sputtered at me, I couldn't call it yelling, grabbed hold of her little frypan and held it up, and I am a small child looking up to where she is standing, looking down at me, holding a knife in her raised hand, angry about something. I have never been hit by this woman. Jean has never put hands on me in anger or discipline and seldom, since I could remember, in demonstrations of love. The child knows then, knew now, that she would not, had no intention to harm me. The child watches, holds it in her heart, as I looked at Jean, my own anger rising into my hands, dropping them, with shock, the words already out—you'd better not try. She was already flinging the frypan clattering into the sink. "I was doing it to myself," she said. And I said—yes, and we met, finally. I peeled carrots and potatoes, too many, laid them in around the roast, thinking Jean would likely throw them out. My hands shook. Jean somewhere else now, feeling her way, pacing the room. "No," she wept, "it will kill me." Her tears filled me just then with unease and irritation. We can find you a place where you don't have to worry about all this, I said, with a wrench of recognition, the *daddy's dead* voice mine now ... *you'll be alright, won't you* .... "I don't worry about it, you do," Jean's voice impassive as she held her stomach and went out on her balcony to sit in her wicker chair, with her back to me, and look at the blue of those mountains showing through the trees. Lost fish and lost time, my mother, my mother, my mother ... sun warm, water mercury blue, clouds are flowing hair across a sky full of light, we are lying on a dock together in our bathing suits, West Hawk Lake, beneath the water the swimmer swims. A returning dream. Something down there trying to kill me, or her—but not anger. Anger demands motion, change, protects.

A cold wind turned English Bay to green froth; clouds over mountains on the north shore slid over them and out of sight. Sun glowered, Sam with me, walking on sand, infinite years muffled by wind on water. Crows, always crows, black, hooded eyes, scavenging. Sam watches the water, the movement of sea on rocks, the spray, birds. Pleased and curious, her retriever's ears rise, eyes bright, tongue pink, mouth open, an animal smile. She watches the sky, keeps an eye on passing boats. Why do she and the crows remind me of my mother? A friend warns I am trying to construct a relationship I never had, that I am allowing compassion for Jean to affect my judgement about what's best. How can compassion be absent from such a judgement? How can it not affect what's best? Love livens spirit, the swimmers swim, below the surface of the waves.

We would go for drives and walks, usually in the cool of the evening, over the remainder of that summer, to Stanley Park, up to Jericho Hill, overlooking English Bay and the mountainous north shore winking its lights across the water, and a city nestled and glowing in evening light. We would park at Spanish Banks to watch the boats, walk a little. We stopped for an ice cream cone or a sundae on the way. These were times when words could flow, suddenly, as music, pictures, feelings, light. What was your father like? I asked Jean. "Scottish," she said, "well educated, didn't like the work of the farm, preferred to write articles for the local paper," she hesitated, said slowly, "I didn't like him very much, he liked himself and his own life, didn't help my mother, left everything for her to do. The boys all left as soon as they could ... they didn't get their lives ... he didn't encourage her, didn't care what we did. It was a poor farm. Others did well. He never made a go of it, didn't like to work." Jean told me they moved into town when she was ten or so. I would learn later why. There, she said, she didn't have to ride Sam the horse to get to school. She became friends with a girl who was "well off," said she didn't know why a girl like Helen would have anything to do with her. I had no knowledge, then, of what Jean as a child and teenager carried of shame and humiliation in that town. She told me she had to work hard to do well in school, that it came easily to Helen, but she didn't work at it, so Jean did better in high school, even though she had been ill, "nothing serious," she said, and had to make up time in summer school in Winnipeg.

"She had a hard time," Jean said of her mother. "No one to help. She would hitch up the horse and buggy, take me and go to neighbours when ... when she needed to." I noticed the pause, an absent beat of something unsaid in our story; hers, Jane's, mine. "I waited for her in the garden," Jean's voice moves in me and I see her lying there between the rows, smelling what grew there in the prairie's dry and dusty heat and sky-bruising rainstorms. Or Jean lying in tall grass, looking at the sky, waiting for Jane, imagining her coming. She told me sometimes she would eat things from those gardens. The two of us there, children in the garden. I sensed what was not said in the spaces between her words, wanted to know more about my grandmother, why the little town where she lived for the rest of her life, after coming from Scotland, made no mention of her by name in their records. I discovered this after I had become curious about my grandmother Jane and her life, and had earlier written away to the town where Jean grew up for whatever history might be there. I would be drawn much deeper, later.

I learned Jean worked in Winnipeg, went to normal school, taught school in little prairie towns during the Depression, but she didn't mention anything about them, except to acknowledge my comment, it must have been difficult, with a simple "Yes." She and my father, a school principal, were married in someone's home in Winnipeg and went north to a little village, she didn't remember its name, "Just marking time there. The man I married," she paused, "your father, had a job there." She didn't speak of what he did, or what happened next, or my birth, or of her taking me to Winnipeg at the outbreak of war in Europe, nothing chronological, until "the place on the river bank" from where I left for Toronto, and where she remained until 1970, when she came west to Vancouver. She didn't mention me, said she "regretted there wasn't more money." My birth, my childhood, her child, me, unspoken.

Jean remembered West Hawk Lake, where we spent all-too-brief stays after the war ended and before my father died, suddenly, as a blood clot lodged in his heart when he stood up from lunch at the boarding house where he stayed during the week, in a small town north of Winnipeg. He had just become principal of a school there that fall. The war had ended by then. Our last time together was the Thanksgiving weekend just before, at West Hawk. What Jean was remembering then I could not tell, the slipstream taking me between here and there, winnowing me pliable as water. October, 1947, another brilliant Manitoba fall. Sky and lake a blue clarity, my father in his best blue suit, white shirt and a tie, changing a flat tire beside the highway on our way to West Hawk Lake, light falling on silvered bulrushes, weeds in the ditch rustling and scraping their podded and veined surfaces against one another. Jean, fretting he'd worn his best clothes for a weekend at the lake, and I am wondering why, as it does not seem that important to a child who does not know yet how adults hide their fear, particularly how Jean hides hers. My father's nosebleeds that summer past would not stop. Later, when we were there, at the lake, I gathered dried wild plants for a grade seven school science project. Jean told me the names of the plants and I was surprised by this revelation of her knowledge, her company. What lost or yet unknown worlds were sensed there? Later my father, who had come and gone from my life for those years of the war, took me walking in darkness towards the lake, down by the side of the highway, cars passing in the night, the stars above us cool and distant, present. He is holding my hand, telling me he "doesn't know what's out there." I didn't know then, or now, if this was a confession, question, or perhaps his parting gift. The darkness around us that night did not have teeth. Then it is the Friday after our weekend at the lake. My father has gone back to Selkirk, the town north of Winnipeg, on the banks of the Red River, where he is the principal of a school. The pot roast Jean cooks after she is home from work on Fridays, when my father returns from Selkirk, is dry, hard like a bone. We wait. Nine pm., the phone rings. Her breathing labours. "Daddy's dead," she tells me. I cannot feel; rather, I notice everything—the gentle, muted quality of her voice, her patience when I forget some task, the orange light in the dial of our battery radio like the moon rising over the slope of her shoulder and back as we lie in bed that night, silent as the radio plays

My father and I, 1939.

organ music, which I cannot abide to this day. I wanted to tell Jean this, but couldn't. Another fall, northern BC, Jean came to visit us. Usually she came by plane, but this time she came on a freighter, through the inside passage north, and along the ninety or so miles of a fiord bathed in October light and watercolour reflections, orange and gold fingers of kelp clinging to granite reaching for the dense green vertical. A woman afraid of the water, of putting her face into it.

On one of our walks, Jean looked up at the city's boulevard trees, talked to a crow that hopped around in front of us, referred to it as "her, she." Crows, I noticed, always seemed to come and light near her. As she talked about the crows gathering and leaving for the winter when she was a child, I recalled again the one story I could recall Jean telling me, from her childhood on the farm, or perhaps in town, "pulling tail feathers of a crow to make it stay the winter." We passed a white sports car parked by the curb. Jean said, "I could buy that. I don't know why I didn't when I was younger. I could have, when I was working." Shy, self-conscious smile, much more than a car, an inexpressible sense of regret, loss. Suddenly there were other stories I had forgotten she'd told me ... money from her chickens' eggs to buy a new dress, until a fox destroyed both eggs and chickens; and taking her father's axe to cut down a young tree for the nest at the top, which she took to school and received first prize, about which she seemed proud ... remembering these now, searching for clues, finding metaphors.

During this time, in August, the psychiatric outreach team from the area's health unit, as I had arranged after the trauma of Jean's encounter with the geriatric assessment unit, came to see Jean in her apartment. The young woman psychiatrist and a psychiatric social worker were pleasant and respectful, chatting with Jean as though they had come for tea. I did talk to her about their coming but she had forgotten. With reassurances and encouragement from me she relaxed and submitted to some of their questions related to neurological function, although she questioned why they were asking her for such information. In familiar surroundings, her own home, and with this sensitive manner of questioning, their assessment of Jean's mental status was as follows: *Jean ... presented as a clean, well-groomed, neatly dressed woman looking much younger than her stated age. She was polite but reserved initially. She became quickly anxious at our questioning and asked repeatedly why we were there even though we answered the question several times. Eye contact was good. Jean herself had no complaints. She appeared euthymic* (mentally tranquil) *objectively. She was in general quite suspicious but there was no continued inappropriate affect.*

Although Jean has expressed some such concerns to her daughter she did not admit to any paranoid ideation today. I specifically enquired into difficulties with her neighbours, the neighbourhood or people stealing things and there was no evidence of delusions at this time or of hallucinations or psychotic thinking. Her speech was normal but she was clearly confabulating. Her score on the mini mental status was 17 out of 30. Her language skills including following of instructions remain quite intact. However her orientation, attention and recall were markedly impaired. She was unable to remember personal data as well such as her age of retirement (my note: at age sixty-five Jean received a government old age security pension but didn't "retire" until age seventy-nine), *the nature of her job when she was working* (my note: Jean worked at a variety of jobs in Vancouver from age sixty-five to seventy-nine, for Office Overload). *Completion of the mini mental state examination was facilitated by the presence of her daughter. At this point there is no way we involuntarily hospitalise....* This assessment took place just weeks after the geriatric assessment unit had tried to commit her to a secure unit at a psychiatric hospital. This outreach team recommended my plan of more support for Jean to remain in her home, until space became available at the care facility where her name was on a waiting list. It was a relief when homemakers came most days, arranged by the outreach psychiatric social worker, who had come with the psychiatrist to do the assessment of Jean in her home. He was a kind and thoughtful man. The term "paranoid ideation," referred to in this assessment, was not what I would have called the confusion Jean could experience seeing someone in her home she didn't recognize, a homemaker, or with finding food left for her and not knowing how it got there. And it would, I think, be logical, in Jean's circumstances, for her to think either it was someone who shouldn't be there, or neighbours who had left things, etc. Labels implying psychosis were not what Jean needed. However, this assessment had at least presented a more balanced picture of Jean and her needs.

Toward the end of summer, Jean appeared to settle. She was letting the homemakers help her more. I was calling her, morning and evening, to help her orient time, and reminding her of when the homemakers were coming, and the Friendship Centre (adult day care) would call for her. She noticed the centre was sending food home with her, and that they were not doing this with everyone. I think she felt embarrassed, perhaps insulted. We continued our walks and drives. As the time drew near for a return to UBC, and the beginning of a two-year writing program, I was trying to see what Jean could manage, uncertain at this point, more conscious of choices narrowing, anxious, and assailed by doubts. Was I able to see what she needed, what would work? Or was I imposing an idea (mine) of what Jean wanted and needed onto her? Was I honest, with her, myself, or was I in denial? What were the essentials? I was feeling isolated, a need for reassurance, was searching for balance, more intuitiveness as to how to go on with my life, and with Jean.

Jean flatly refused to go to a picnic the Friendship Centre had organized, called me in tears late afternoon, to tell me she couldn't manage to get anything to eat, and was frying an egg and had a half a slice of bread on a plate, when I arrived. She carefully wrapped a tea towel around the metal handle of her small frypan to bring it to the table, where she set it down on another neatly folded tea towel. Her blouse was partly undone, cuffs unbuttoned. She was careful to turn off her stove, as she always was. "Just wanting to talk," she said was why she called, "don't need any help." I asked why she didn't want to go to the Friendship Centre. Jean muttered she "hasn't long to live, wants some choice," then added that she couldn't get ready by herself. I suggested some clothes and offered to come by the next morning to help her get ready. She seemed to think this was okay. The next day she was ready when I arrived, dressed in something altogether different from what I had laid out for her, making her own completely appropriate choice, had already made and eaten her oatmeal porridge for breakfast and was putting things in and out of her purse, trying to figure out if she had enough money to pay for her lunch, and whether she needed her bus pass, where her keys were, etc., trying to get some order into her mind about what she needed to do. Said, exasperated, she "hates the place (the Friendship Centre) and doesn't know why she's going." I finally left her sitting on her bed with her purse, told her she was okay, she had some money, everything was fine, made her a cup of tea to drink while she waited to be picked up. When I called her that evening she was in a good mood, seemed to have had a nice time—an outing for a walk "down by the river" she said, and "they got me home okay."

I had arranged for homemakers to buy food on account at the local supermarket and explained this to Jean many times, but she did not like the idea of "strangers buying stuff she doesn't need." Her primary homemaker was discreet, thoughtful and kind, but also purposeful. I hoped this would work, but found I would often need to bring over food. The fear of not having enough money was always there for Jean. By this time, I had been ghosting in and out of my writing program, unable to write much other than the basic minimum required. I was also teaching in the night school program a couple of evenings per week, and still coping with my hypersensitive immune system and its reactions to various exposures. Grieving, tired, angry with myself for feeling that my life was on hold when Jean was fighting for hers and this might be the fight of her life, I arrived at Jean's one day, tense and angry, and we had an argument, which upset and confused Jean. I felt terrible. I talked to her about a care facility. She listened as I mentioned the advantages. This time, this moment, Jean appeared interested, but worried about her money, "is there enough for this?" I reassured her there was. She was willing to "take a look, just to see, no rush." I said, no rush, we'll just go have a look at it. And I spoke to her about the care facility, but not that her name was on its wait-list, and feared she would hate me for what would be coming.

Then Jean seemed more clear, went out shopping, to the bank, seemed to want to take charge again. She had continued to get her hair done, always remembering to pay, they told me, when I came to bring her home. They laughed and giggled because she sang to herself while under the hair dryer. Although they meant no harm, I found myself resenting their amusement. Her primary homemaker, who had been with her for some time, was phoning regularly at this point, to let me know how things were going. She mentioned Jean had told her all about me "going to school and riding my bicycle." Jean had also been asking me how things were going for me and what my work was like. The horizon of our life together seemed to be expanding, like that vast encircling prairie circumference, sparse, concealing, surprising, linking land with sky, taking the eye beyond itself. Winter solstice was approaching. It was difficult to see Jean trying so hard to stay where she was, in her familiar place. I asked Jean—what if you become sick? She believed she would simply go to hospital if she was ill. I tried to explain that, under those circumstances, she would not have any choice, other than the next available space in the system. I had seen where, what that could be.

Fear and Bullies

Until December, 1991, I had very little contact with Jean's regular physician. The past few months I had begun accompanying her to her appointments with him. I had not gone into his office with her, but had seen, and experienced, the pattern of her unwillingness to have go to these appointments, made by his office for her, and her agitated state for some time after being there, reminiscent of the geriatric assessment unit experience. December 24, I delivered a letter to this doctor's office, prior to his seeing Jean at her next appointment on December 27. My letter explained that I had been advised an emergency placement for Jean might be coming available within weeks, but not in the facility for which her name was wait-listed, where I had understood there would not be an opening for some time to come. I did not want to impose two moves on Jean, nor the possibility of losing her position on the wait-list for the facility of choice. There would be little time to prepare Jean for this transition. Jean's doctor, on several occasions, had expressed his opinion that I "ought to put her in a nursing home," which did not give me a lot of confidence regarding his general sensitivity in this matter. So my letter to him was very careful about describing the difficulty

Jean was having with making a move to a care facility, so that he might raise the issue with her and talk with her about the advantages of such a move, with a view to helping her accept it. I wanted Jean to hear this from someone else, as well as from me. Although her doctor had never involved himself in any of the arrangements I made for Jean with the health unit, nor had he seemed to recognize Jean could only afford to be in a government-subsidized facility, for which there were long wait-lists, I thought by giving him this letter ahead of time, with the background details, his approach would be sensitized. I gave him names to contact for further information, if he wished, suggested I thought it would help if Jean heard it from him as well as myself, but that if he felt he was unable to advise her, he could let me know. I heard nothing from either the doctor or his office.

Once there for her appointment, I went into the examining room with Jean. This doctor's first and only words, directed at Jean, was a brusque "get on the scale," followed by, "get off the scale," after which, wordless, he pulled up her arm and literally wrenched off her jacket with no request at all or intimation that he wanted it removed. I saw, heard, the stethoscope thump against her scarred chest as he listened to her heart. He pulled over a high stool to sit on, looked down at Jean, held out my letter and asked me if I had discussed with my mother the particular space that had come available on an emergency basis. I said, no, not specifically, that I had hoped for a more *discreet* raising of the issue at this time, hoping he would realize, as discussed in the letter, how the immediacy could panic her. But from his perch on the stool two feet or so in front of her, he expressed his anger with me, saying: "Oh, I see, you're passing the buck to me, fine, just fine, thanks a lot." I motioned to him, hoping he would see my alarm at the effect his words and manner were having on Jean. He then spoke to her directly, using some of the language and ideas I had expressed in the letter, but adding a number of blunt suggestions, such as (to me) "a need for nursing supervision to take her pills." When Jean finally asked if she "was being forced to do this," his reply was "well, if you go home and find all your furniture gone, that's one way to make a choice." Jean had turned to me, saying "this isn't right" while I was rendered momentarily speechless by the shock of what had happened. The doctor stood then, said, "I'll leave you two girls to fight it out," and left the room, calling, "bye," from down the hall and left the door to the room, where we were, open to a reception room full of waiting people, while Jean was left attempting to talk to me in a completely agitated state. A letter of complaint from myself to the BC College of Physicians and Surgeons resulted in a one-sentence letter of apology from this physician, from whom I severed all further connection.

January 1992 there was a call from this physician's office, requesting I pick up a medical history for Jean which needed to be delivered to the facility that could take Jean as an emergency placement. The envelope, containing what was referred to as Jean's medical history, had been left unsealed. I was chilled by its contents. The portion of her history as written by this doctor included, among his comments, that Jean had "major non-compliance with medications ... paranoia, hostility and suspicion...." There were also copies of a discharge summary and a psychiatric assessment report about Jean, and, to my surprise, about myself, compiled by the geriatric assessment unit several months ago, after Jean's brief attendance and subsequent refusal to continue. The agencies I had been dealing with in regard to Jean's ongoing care, and her doctor, as well as those with whom I would be working in the future, including whatever care facility in which Jean would finally become a resident, had received, or would receive, copies of these reports. As it had been several months since these reports had been circulated, their damage had been done. I began to understand the changed attitude of many of the individuals within these agencies with whom, to now, I had been working to find ways for Jean to remain supported in her home. Some individuals had remained supportive, most were very guarded with me, a few were cold to hostile.

The geriatric assessment unit's discharge summary and psychiatric assessment were two separate reports, each prepared by different people. Comments contained in them characterized me as *uncooperative and difficult* and suggested I had put my mother's safety at risk. The discharge summary was written by a doctor, who, as he indicated in the report, was not present in the unit at any time when Jean was there, had never met her, or myself, nor had he attended the unit's conference with my son and myself regarding Jean. From an assortment of notes made by others, it appeared he had put together a profile of Jean and myself. He wrote, at one point in the report, that Jean was discharged because the unit was unable to convince me of *the need for long term placement, that I had difficulty cooperating with the evaluation and management process and did not agree with the evaluation of my mother's need for placement.* He was apparently unaware of the fact that, before

Jean's contact with the unit, I had already toured facilities and put her name on the waiting list for a specific care facility of choice and had informed the unit of this at the conference he did not attend. What this doctor euphemistically referred to in this report as *Long Term Care placement*, was in fact, as members of the unit, the psychiatrist, and the head nurse indicated, *having Jean certified and committed involuntarily to a secure unit in a mental hospital, Riverview*. He was likely also unaware of the mental health outreach assessment done in Jean's home a few weeks after this attempt to commit her, which concluded, *at this point there is no way that we involuntarily hospitalise* (Jean), which provided another perspective on this doctor's further statement that Jean was *at significant risk in the community*. This doctor stated that Jean's discharge from the unit was *without addressing home safety, financial competence, etc.,* due to what he referred to as my *lack of cooperation*. Again, he was unaware these matters were all discussed rather fully at the conference, where I had indicated I had been taking on these issues for Jean, as circumstances developed. There had even been a letter from the unit's psychiatrist, who seemed to lead the conference, sent to me after her phone call to me, when I had again refused to have Jean involuntarily committed. In the letter she stated that since speaking with me "they had a better idea of how Jean was managing at home and realized she behaved differently in her familiar surroundings...." At the conference, I had said it was my intention that Jean remain in her home with increased home support until such time as space became available in a care facility, allowing her as much choice as possible, which was subsequently supported by the psychiatric outreach assessment from her area health unit a few weeks later, when they interviewed Jean in her own home. None of this was made clear in this report. Another serious allegation appearing in this report was a vague statement: *it was not possible usefully to address the problem of medication compliance because of difficulties with the family....* What was being implied here? I was beginning to recognize and be deeply angered by this recurring self-protective pattern of placing blame outside the system, both bureaucratic and professional, as well as very harmful profiling that had an impact on Jean's rights, profiling that I felt would only continue and worsen as it built on this foundation of what were considered professional records.

Included with this discharge report was a psychiatric assessment, written by a resident in psychiatry. It contained statements that ranged from careless to the bizarre and dangerous. There were references to the inappropriateness of Jean living on the fifth floor of her apartment building, when, in fact, she lived on the main floor of a two-storey structure, close to front and back doors and the laundry room. Her apartment number was in the 500's, but an occupational therapist from the unit had actually visited Jean in her home. The resident intern commented: *the patient developed inappropriate behaviour....* but did not indicate what that behaviour was, until later in the report when there was a note: *sometimes resists homemakers.* The report added that Jean *thought her food was being poisoned.* I do not recall Jean ever saying this. To my knowledge, she simply thought various homemakers who were sent to her home might not wash their hands properly and she could get sick. Was she asked a leading question at some point—*do you think people are poisoning you?* Were words suggested to her, put into her mouth? Given Jean's difficulty finding the right word, any so-called *paranoiac ideation, hallucination or psychosis* ascribed to her were more likely simply lost words and their meanings. But, as I was discovering, psychiatric interpretation and labelling based on theories of abnormality could lose all common sense.

Under the heading of *Recommendations* was written: *a suggestion has been done to the daughter to try to shop for some food and leave it in the fridge for her mother.* I had, of course, been shopping and preparing food for Jean for a couple of years prior to this. I was astounded to find in this report a notation about *Past Family Psychiatric History.* Since there wasn't one, I was even more astounded that under this heading the resident intern wrote the following: (Jean's) *daughter has been treated for depression after a divorce.* I read it again. Jean and I happen to have never been treated for depression, and have never had any contact with psychiatrists or psychiatric medication at any time in our lives. Where had this come from? Had information I had given to the unit's psychiatric social worker that I had sought counselling a year after my divorce, when I was completing a university degree, working part time, beginning to feel Jean's growing needs, as well as my own, translated into being "treated for depression"? This statement required immediate correction, because it was false, and had dangerous implications for Jean, implying that depression might run in the family, tracing it back to her; that electroshock treatment could be deemed "necessary."

There was little I could do to undo the damage these reports had already done, other than to write letters immediately to all members of the unit with whom I had met at that conference last summer, pointing out the errors and requesting immediate corrections be sent to all those agencies and individuals concerned, and that the original uncorrected reports be withdrawn and destroyed. I pointed out the editorial underlining of negative references to myself contained in the reports and asked, by whom? and why? I pointed out that, if it was done by someone receiving these reports then it indicated a biased profile of myself given to persons I had worked with, and would need to be working with in the future. My letters were sent January 3, 1992. I received a reply from the unit's director, who, in her letter, took responsibility for the errors, as she stated, "for having made a bad decision to ask someone, who had not been involved with the unit to do the discharge summary report ... as a result of the administrative decision made, mis-communication occurred ... have learned to make certain only people who are directly involved write such reports...." She indicated she would send copies of a revised report to all those agencies and persons involved.

But the damage had already been done. Both corrected and uncorrected reports would be found in Jean's files until she died. The corrected report remained negative, however, about Jean's future, as one of *continuing deterioration, that her psychiatric evaluation revealed significant problems with memory and judgement, clouded by paranoia,* yet admits mental status examinations were not performed. A young activity worker with the unit had, in the discharge report, written subjective opinions on Jean's *passivity with respect to participation and socialization,* based on her observation that Jean *seemed to shy away from socialization with other clients and staff and did not elaborate very much during her conversations, but was pleasant when anyone addressed her... did join in the Opportunity Group, Survival Cooking, Outings, Exercises and Dear Abby, but she always appeared bored or uninterested during groups....* Perhaps she was, simply, uninterested. My attempts to provide a perspective of Jean as a very independent woman who had lived alone most of her life was, in these records, and would continue to be pathologized, and she would be characterized as *suspicious ... hostile ... paranoiac ...* This activity worker then offered further opinions as to why Jean was unfocused and not able to follow directions and finally suggested perhaps Jean would be better in a *one-on-one situation,* without any apparent awareness that her suggestion would certainly qualify all her previously stated observations and the opinions she drew from them.

With regard to the psychiatric assessment report and its errors, the reply from the unit's psychiatrist came later, in March 1992, and suggested the comments I took issue with in her report were meant to be "supportive to both you and your mother." On the issue of the inclusion of a past family psychiatric history, she agreed, "your own counselling was given to us incorrectly. I, too, find this highly significant (i.e., we are on the lookout for depression as it runs in families in some cases) and have corrected this accordingly...." She indicated she did not know who did the underlining of the references to myself, stating, "it is often done by health care professionals who receive the reports," and went on to say, "I agree with you that the mis-information in the reports is serious and must be corrected ... felt personally disappointed that this has occurred since I enjoyed meeting you and your son in the family meeting (team conference). I know that I clearly outlined my philosophy to you regarding my policy of helping people to potentiate their care giving goals, regardless of whether we agree with them or not. I still believe that, and practise accordingly, and I admire your resolve to do what you felt best for your mother...." She expressed surprise that a copy of her report became available to me, "... my psychiatric reports are confidential and should be available only to myself and to other significant health care professionals involved. Only upon informed consent (her underlining) of my patients should anyone else gain access to them. My reports often contain information about patients' concerns, thoughts or past experiences, which patients do not wish their relatives to know about. Fortunately this was not the case with this consultation My comments are addressed not so much to you, but to the person who provided you with copies. I hope you have an opportunity to discuss this with him or her...." This psychiatrist carried out no interviews with Jean. Two years after this, when Jean's records were misread, putting her in danger, once again, of electroshock treatments, I wrote back to this psychiatrist and received her letter back, this time indicating what had been omitted from her previous letter. She said, "... legally I am not permitted to delete the original information ... I have added an annotation which states that your mother has no family psychiatric history ... anyone ... will read this addendum...." I was left wondering how our seemingly straightforward comments may be interpreted, taken out of context, distorted and placed in records with labels that follow us through the health care system as definitive truth, a medical or psychiatric history to suit purposes purporting to be in our best interests. Would expressing concern about this then be seen as *paranoiac ideation?* The shadow of the bully is fear. Jean was teaching me about the bully in me, and how systemic bullying happens.

Shades of grey, the January day we drove to East Vancouver to view an emergency placement for Jean. It was a very long way from both our homes on the west side of Vancouver. The building was small, clean, well kept, wedged between two merging major traffic routes. Its interior walls were a darker shade of blue that did not encourage optimism. I could tell Jean was not comfortable. It was suggested to me that I leave her for a few hours on her own. On my return, I was told Jean had sworn at them and wanted to leave, confused as to where I had gone. Big surprise, I wanted to say, but said nothing, nodded, and took her back home, wondering, if we turned this down, would she lose her place on the wait-list for the facility, not of her choice, but mine? When I got home, there was a message on my answering machine telling me the space available for her at the care facility I had picked for her "will be given to someone else if she doesn't want it." I called, perplexed as to why they'd left such a message, since I had been told nothing would be available until at least the following summer, and was informed the space had been available since before Christmas. No one had contacted me. The need for a decision was now immediate.

When I brought Jean to view the facility, several minutes' drive from Jean's home, she responded positively. The building was new, appeared well laid out, its interior walls light and bright. There were sun rooms at the end of each hallway extending north, south, east, and west from a central nursing station on the two upper floors, which accommodated a resident population of over two hundred. The main floor was wide, with many windows, a pleasant dining room and lounge, with a gas fireplace. There was also a small library, garden, and a small hair-dressing salon. Jean seemed at ease. The person who showed us around described how the facility could meet her needs for privacy, community, and health support, if needed.

Later, we sat outside her apartment in my car and talked, or I did, reiterating what we had seen and been told at the facility and suggesting she could try it out, that we could keep her apartment for a couple of months and see how it goes. She said she "might try it out," and I felt it was the best I could hope for. Her feelings could change, this conversation forgotten. But something seemed to have shifted, and I felt relief, sudden optimism that, at some level, Jean could be coming to terms with this in her own way. I wanted to believe I was not forcing her to go where she didn't want to, but I knew deeper still that in that moment I had become the child, and Jean the parent sensing my need, my helplessness, and was in some way responding to this. I had no idea how we would get from here to there.

During the two weeks until Jean's move into the care facility, I had been spending increasing amounts of time with her and avoiding any packing. The facility had indicated what could be brought with her. It would be minimal. They suggested their furniture, but I thought her own familiar furniture would help her to orient herself, with less anxiety. I had arranged with my son and daughter-in-law to move her things into her room while Jean was being seen by the facility's director of admissions, so that she would find familiar pieces, her dressers and chair, her lamps and TV and the pictures I did for her in pastels, a view of the Assiniboine River in Winnipeg, from the window where we lived, and the October forest of West Hawk Lake, where we spent, in my mind, idyllic moments, and with them, the watercolour she had of a Scottish moor with crows lifting into sky. The bed was hospital-type, provided by the facility, her own bedding and quilt would be in place on it, her clothing in her drawers and cupboard. I hoped it would provide her some easement; it could do the opposite. Back at home, preparing a meal for myself, I saw my father, there in my mind, remembered how, after he had died, I had a sense of him *there*, able to see me, an absent presence that seemed to impel me to get on with my life. As I cut up salad for my lunch, I was with him again, walking together down Portage Avenue on a warm summer Saturday night. A drunk soldier had lunged out a doorway at us, yelling. My father was holding my hand and I was not afraid. The soldier suddenly smiled, lurched past. "She'll be alright now, you'll be alright, I've been watching over you." These words seemed at that moment to come from the comforting presence of my father

When I sat down to my lunch, I was back on a Greyhound Bus, with my mother. We were going to Selkirk, just north of Winnipeg, where my father had just died, so my mother could speak with his doctor, find out what had happened to my father. We sat at the very back of the bus. I had a chocolate milkshake in the bus depot before we left, and that, and the fumes from the bus engine made me feel ill, the passing fields, the light there hurt my eyes. I waited for my mother while she went into the doctor's office. It seemed a long time. The halls there were dark, shiny dark brown linoleum hurt my eyes. I went into the bathroom, threw up, and put cold wet towels over my eyes. I was having my first migraine. The time of my father's death was noon, he was just getting up from lunch, my mother told me. That day of his dying, I had come home from school to have lunch, alone in our rooms on Osborne Street, and had begun to practise my singing lesson, which I almost never did. How my parents had managed to give me private singing lessons and why, I would never know, but I was extremely shy, would not sing in front of anyone, frustrating my teacher to the point of discontinuing my private lessons. Group lessons were worse, and that was that. But this day, the day, even the time, it seemed, of my father's heart stopping, without knowing why, I began to sing as I had never sung. A voice just came out from me free and full of unusual joy and feeling. When my mother told me the time of my father's death I stored away some childish guilt I felt, never sang like that again. As I had my lunch, memory dissolved time, and guilt, fed me instead with a sense of connection, that what had been, was still.

Profiles

It is a violation of my natural external freedom, not to be able to go where I please ... my personality is wounded by such experiences, because my most immediate identity rests in my body.
                                                              —Hegel.

Prior to Jean's entering the intermediate care facility, it was suggested to me, by the facility's director, that a very large dose of loxapine (an anti-psychotic drug used in care facilities) could be given Jean "to get her in here," which, she added, "could then be tapered down to an ongoing dose as needed." Declining this was another skirmish with the bureaucratic priority that took precedence over, ignored, the impairment associated with these neuroleptic drugs and the risks involved with their use, particularly in older persons. Jean was now eighty-eight.

One of the requirements contained in the Residential Care Manual covering the quality of care at such government-subsidized facilities indicates: "Restraints (defined as any physical, mechanical or chemical means for controlling the behaviour or limiting the freedom of any resident) will be used only after all reasonable alternatives have been explored and will be the least restrictive type possible and that in a situation of imminent danger to self or other which cannot be managed in an alternate fashion, the decision to impose restraint will be made by the nurse in charge and that a physician's order, normally required prior to restraint be obtained within 72 hours of restraint."

As her clothing and furniture were being moved into her room by my son and daughter-in-law, Jean and I sat with the director of admissions. After an hour's interview with us, the interviewer wrote the following profile: *sense of taste, touch and smell fair. skin good, mouth fair, ambulation good, eating and dressing skills independent. mental status: cooperation very limited, suspicious—she thinks to answer any questions is not necessary, she is not ill. Tries to cover up her memory deficit. status of comprehension: restless, not answering some questions, denies any problems, insis* (insists) *she is able to managing* (manage) *well and don't* (doesn't) *need any help*

Jean's memory was indicated as *poor* for recent events and *fair* for long term, with the comment: *thinking about the farm and animals, short periods of time, then gets angry, why I'm asking her .... emotional status: restive, suspicious, hostile or angry at times, no insight—no adequate judgement....* I did not see any anger expressed by Jean during that interview. It is unclear to me how Jean's being asked about the farm where she grew up translated to Jean *thinking about the farm and animals.* No adequate judgement? I would suggest that Jean had the good sense (judgement) to perceive and understand the true nature of the situation (insight) which made her restive (impatient with restraint, control). When asked if Jean "wanders" I said no. The interviewer wrote: *risk to elop* (elope). Other comments by this interviewer were: *client has very short interest span, poor orientation and attention, sight poor, hearing good, very independent* (I had indicated Jean's need for independence). Jean had already been set up as *difficult to manage,* by the medical history supplied by her former doctor to this facility, and from that original geriatric assessment discharge report, which has not been destroyed but, unknown to me until after her death, had been kept in her file by this care facility, along with the "corrected" report, and would remain there for the duration of her residency. Her former doctor did not indicate any basis for suggesting *chronic organic brain disease* or an *arteriosclerotic heart.* His comment to me after a CT scan he had ordered the previous fall had been that there was *no evidence of any organic brain deterioration.* The blood work required for admission to this care facility indicated Jean's blood digoxin under this physician's care to be at a level of 1.8nmol./l, which was at, or over, the accepted limit of safety, according to several sources in medical literature. Jean's sensitivity to Aspirin, her mastectomy, and GI bleed did not appear to be included in the admission record, nor was there an indication that Jean had a lens implant, or the implications of this in terms of her need to wear dark glasses in sunlight, or the fact that there was a time lag, going from areas of different lighting, for her vision to adjust, that this alone would be a source of confusion, disorientation, or that she used eye drops for glaucoma. There was nothing positive written about Jean.

What if Jean had been viewed from a collaborative and validating perspective, and seen to be acting with strength, a survivor claiming her right to autonomy, to not be interrogated in an authoritatively aggressive, intrusive and disempowering manner? Under interrogation by strangers and in the absence of Jean's ability to immediately find the words she needed to articulate what she was feeling, and with a lack of real information about her, subjective assumptions were readily made, along with impositions of personal bias, prejudice, and just plain attitude. The word *respect* used so frequently in the public relations of this particular care facility, which first attracted me to consider it as home for Jean, would become just that, a word, requiring qualification—respect under what circumstances?

Jean's records during her residence at this facility, I discovered only after her death, demonstrated something else, a pattern that begged answers to a question of whose hostility, paranoia, whose aggression was underlying the various systemic and individual reactions to her that Jean encountered while a resident here. Assumptions were made about her, and interpretations of her actions and speech that ignored common sense and reflected the needs of a particular assessment. These were made without qualification or explanation, such as consideration of the effects on Jean of illness, fatigue, inappropriate drugs, environment, and the attitudes and behaviour of those providing care for Jean.

What would the effect have been on Jean's care, on who she was seen as, if, instead of *paranoiac, hostile and suspicious,* she had been described as cautious, self-protective, private, preserving her dignity? Jean was following her natural instincts, normal in these circumstances, by being cautious, protective and private, and resisting, described in any dictionary as *resisting the authorities, especially in a conquered or enemy-occupied territory.*

We had completed the admissions process, were in what would be Jean's room, the size of it somewhat smaller than a clean, no-frills motel room. She did not look around as I pointed out a covered courtyard patio where we could put some shelving for a garden just outside, under her window. She sank down on the bed, hands covering her eyes— "I didn't think my life would come to this," her anguished cry, despair; and mine. There was nothing I could find to say or do, and feared she would not see me as an ally, which at this point was more important than ever, I thought, for her, and for me. In desperation I reminded her of her apartment, still rented for two months, that she could see how she liked it here, knowing, both of us did, she would never go back there again.

In the emotional jungle I passed through time and time again, as I went on this journey with Jean, both anger and fear could become either enemy or friend, depending on my recognition of them, letting them bring me back to focus, direction, action, so that emotional fracturing, or the threat of it, became the source of a more instinctive, intuitive means of continuing on, both in my own life and with Jean.

Quick Read Fox

I spent much of the time with Jean those first two weeks, hoping to ease the transition, to interpret the facility to Jean and Jean to the staff, was told at one point, "some days she doesn't even mention you," at another, "your mother is adjusting as well as we can expect. She will be disoriented, her sense of time and space, her memory already impaired will become worse, until she settles in ... when you take her out for drives and bring her back here she won't remember who we are, or where she is, but let us worry about that ...." Her records indicated on the third day of her residence in the facility Jean *appears anxious, wringing hands, pleasant, but stated she's not pleased at all to be here, that she changed her mind about moving "this place is not for her ... wants to be on her own..." does not want to be around 'these people' Appears to be an elopement risk ... packing her clothes and wishes to leave. calmed down by staff for a short period of time. Consistently wanting to go home. Daughter informed—to call her if necessary....*

From midnight to 7:00 a.m. Jean was described in her records as *restless, confused, short-tempered ... sore elbow, lump red and sore ... awake, restless, wanting to go home, pacing hallway aimlessly....* I arrived later that morning. No one mentioned anything to me about a sore elbow or red lump or her restless night. When she was changing her blouse, I saw that the benign lump that had been on her left elbow for several years was now very red and swollen, and a red line under her skin extended out from the lump. The infection had come on suddenly. Because lymph nodes had been taken from her underarm when her left breast was removed in 1988, Jean had to be very careful of any infection on this arm. I spoke with a nurse about having it looked at by a doctor right away. He smiled pleasantly and said they "will keep an eye on it and let a doctor know if they think it necessary." When I referred to her mastectomy, he was unable to find any record of it in her charts. I could see there was no point in pursuing this with him and, instead, found the director of nursing in her office, who came immediately to look at Jean's arm and agreed Jean needed to go right away to the emergency of a nearby hospital, where the growth was lanced and treated by a physician, who remained silent during the whole procedure, saying to me when he was finished, "You got here just in time." I didn't know if it was approval or an accusation. The director of nursing noted this event in Jean's records as: *L. elbow red, inflamed and infected looking mass 1" diam., L. arm around mass red and swollen.* Later that day, Jean was described as pacing the hallway aimlessly and more settled that night, her arm, the next day as *reddened down forearm,* the last and only reference to her arm. The sixth day in this facility Jean was described as *settling slowly and socialising, the theme of most conversation: this not her home and her desire to be on her own—not so upset when talking about this.* The seventh day, Jean's own writing appears in her records:

Records for the seventh to eleventh day described Jean: *pleasant on contact, no show of anxiety nor expressed wish to be on her own, pleasant, appears comfortable....* On the eighteenth day, a note appears: *when asked if she likes the food she says "I'm not a fussy person, but I don't mean by that that it's not good— its quite alright ..."* knows she has been here a few weeks, happy....

It was early to mid-March before there were any more entries in Jean's records and these referred to the problem she had with care aides coming into her room in the middle of the night to check on her and waking her up. Two days after this complaint, she went outside the building to walk, recorded as AWOL, from which she returned, it was noted, with *no incident*. It was noted she *appears quite restless and agitated*, without indicating whether this was before or after leaving the building. Shortly thereafter another note appeared in her records: *loves to walk outside ... walking program? "I like to walk by myself" Walking program starts in the summer.*

Spring in the sky over Jericho Beach, eagles circling against thunderclouds high over a running tide of salmon, herring, the eulachon, hidden under a grey and broken ocean surface. Jean's appearance, her surface protection was breaking down, the elegant dresser still there in the cut and style of her clothes, her walk erect, tall, graceful—but her clothing now in some disarray, creased, hair falling into her eyes, bruises on her forehead and shins from unfamiliar edges, doors no longer where they were, not leading where they used to. Chronology and location, here and there, now called into question by Jean's mind, as a leaf floating into shadows, crevices, gaps, and emerging, colours more vibrant than they were before. This so-called "deteriorated" woman, as from long frozen sleep, spontaneously and warmly took her grandson's arm in affection, told him he was handsome.

Inexplicably, one day, it was all I could do to keep my anger in check when someone from the facility called me and put Jean on the phone to talk to me. I had a phone installed in her room, and had been calling her regularly, as well as going to be with her as much as I could. This unexpected call brought on such unanticipated, disconcerting anger, so inappropriate, I realized I no longer knew what being free meant. For Jean or myself. Written in my journal for this day in spring:

I want to weep and cannot
for loss of grief
grief grief why
anger shakes me
pain that can't be touched

There were a cluster of dreams. In the first, I watch myself drowning in a lake with a rocky shore. Someone runs down to save me and then appears before me alternately crying and smiling, and I don't know if I'm dead or alive. In another, Jean is standing on some stone steps leading up to a large, square house that belongs to a friend. She, Jean, wants a particular music record, is saying what she would like, but I can't hear her, and then I am filling up small bags with earth so that I can run and carry them at the same time.

Jean pulled flowers from the garden outside her window overlooking a patio open to the sky, from the pots of zinnias, pansies, geraniums, roses, dahlias, petunias, and asters—her favourite, she once told me—her mother had planted them in her garden. I planted them in containers, arranged them on shelving I bought at a lumber yard. She brought the flowers to her room, dirt still clinging to them, sometimes propped them in a glass, or I would find them collapsed and limp in the corners of the window sill and drawers, in her pockets. I was thinking of Jane, her garden, where Jean went to be with her mother, and the flowers Jane planted around the house Jean had described, when memory carried her words as an ocean slipping over its shore, a river seeking its destination. Jean left her mother's garden behind, and later her own, along the fence in that yard where I had my meeting with the snake, and my father lifted me up onto the roof of an old shed and threw up a large red beach ball for me to catch and I thought it was a sun bouncing along the edge of my own world. There were gardens since, but they were mine, the earliest, when we still lived in rooms on Osborne Street. I had no access to a garden so was given a plot at Girl Guide House, to pass a badge. I failed my badge, and tried again the next summer, this time tending more carefully my prescribed rows of zinnias, cornflowers, marigolds, carrots, beets, and beans. Later, in high school and university, I found myself drawn to the river bank, behind our new home, grew roses there, first, then more, until, when I left for Toronto, other residents had joined in and the river's flank bloomed. I did not know then, where this had come from, left it behind. It would be a very long time before I would garden again.

It was already May, and I was to be leaving soon for a trip with my daughter to France. My first holiday in several years. I was excited and looking forward to seeing my daughter again and having this time together, but apprehensive about Jean. Was it too soon, would I be abandoning her here without an advocate? Forms needed to be dealt with, whether or not Jean was to be resuscitated by "heroic measures" in the event of critical illness, and burial arrangements. Jean had never spoken of her death, or her wishes. I did not really know what Jean would want and my sense was this might be too vulnerable a time to raise this with her, but this may have had more to do with my own fears. I requested what I thought she would want, which was perhaps simply what I would prefer in the same situation ... no heroic measures, the opportunity for her to die without being kept alive beyond her body's natural capacity, and to die with dignity in her own place, here, in her room at the care facility, if possible. I chose cremation and made arrangements for both of us, feeling cremation more freeing than being buried underground, the thought of which always produced claustrophobia in me. I never did discuss this with her during the traumatic journey ahead, guided more by the past than the future.

The staff encouraged me to go off on my holiday and not to worry, told me, "She will be fine." I wrote a letter for their files, describing numerous things I thought would assist the staff in knowing what to do for her, that would help Jean feel more at home and avoid confrontation and misunderstanding. Just before I was about to leave, someone from the care facility called to tell me there has been what they referred to as "an incident." Facility records, which I only had access to after Jean's death, described this event as: *Resident went outside. Attempting to help get her back from the building, resident started to get aggressive confused violent combative and kicking the nurse and scratched nurse both arm* (arms). *Unable to get her back in the building. Called for help and R.D., R.N. assisted resident get back in the building & taken back to room. Resident remains aggressive, confused and hitting the nurse, throwing books & binders from the nursing station. Striking at staff ....* At this point Jean's doctor, since she entered the care facility, was called, as well as myself. He was not available. An on-call doctor came, in about an hour, to examine Jean. This doctor stated in her note: *known paranoid dementia but is not usually violent. Blood pressure higher than normal and a pulse rate of 104, with atrial fibrillation, an irregular heart beat....* and suggested that a transient ischemic attack causing disorientation, confusion could be one reason for the episode. She wrote an order for Haldol, an anti-psychotic, but instructed it *to be given only if there is a repeat episode,* after I suggested that Jean may simply have had a desire to walk, that it was something that had always been important to her. Jean's records indicated that just prior to this *incident*, Jean had complained of care staff coming in to check on her in the middle of the night and waking her and she was having trouble getting back to sleep. The most significant factor at this time, in my opinion, other than possible lack of sleep, was that the care worker who went to bring Jean back to the facility initiated a confrontation by taking hold of Jean and trying to force her to return. I had occasion to speak with this member of staff at the time and found her tense, with little to say. There were bruises on Jean's arms and hands, which the staff suggested to me were "normal" for a person of her age. Jean did not have bruises like that, from normal contact. Nothing was mentioned in Jean's records about this bruising, nor any connection made to the effect of interrupted sleep or the approach of care workers.

It is normal and instinctive for a physically active person to want to take a walk in the fresh air and this was a lifetime habit of Jean's. The record of this *incident* also failed to indicate that Jean had gone out before, on two prior occasions and, her records stated, *returned without incident*, or to refer to that other note that appeared earlier in her file: *loves to walk outside ... walking program? "I like to walk by myself" ... walking program starts in the summer ....* In future, any walks Jean might have attempted (there are very few) are referred to as *wandered away*. The evidence contained in these records was that Jean had indicated she liked to walk, and that no walking program was ever implemented for her. Other than the walks and drives we took together, Jean could only get to her garden on the patio, which was open to the air, or to a small garden off the dining area on the main floor, ringed with a wall high fence. To characterize this need to walk as eloping or wandering denied common sense and normal needs for physical exercise to restore a sense of well-being and balance. Jean showed every sign of coming to terms with living at the facility, as earlier records of her first two months there indicated. While I was away for the month of June there were no further recorded notes other than: *apparently no further outbursts Haldol* (an anti-psychotic) *not being used.*

And in Jean's handwriting:

which was followed by a note: *pulse 110 . irreg.* The same day this was entered, an order was written for the anti-psychotic loxapine, to be given as needed for what was termed *striking out*. There was no indication in her records whether this loxapine was given. Near the end of the month, this appeared in her records, written by Jean.

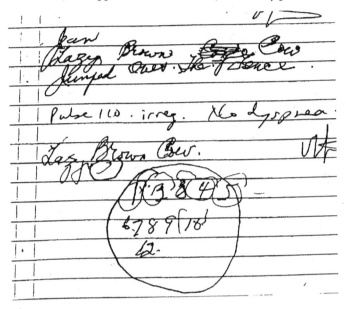

Summer, 1992, and home from France, I was told Jean was refusing to be bathed, that she would "not go to hairdresser." Her records for that time contained a note: *Jean's dementia is not any worse, but she is also difficult w. eye drops and heart medication on occasion. She has asked after her daughter/home etc. once recently but quickly forgot same.* When I began assisting care aides with Jean's bath, a number of problems were apparent. The tub was threatening. The care aides spoke loudly, were tense, appeared to think Jean didn't know what she wanted. They hadn't figured out that when rushed, Jean said "too hot" sometimes, when she meant, "too cold." Jean was not allowed to determine what part of her would be washed and when. I pointed these things out, suggested placing a chair in a shower, but care aides rotated constantly. Some made a point of coming to me and telling me they had no problems at all with Jean.

Over the summer Jean, Sam, and I continued our walks. It was mid-August. Under our feet there were leaves, dry, and fallen already. An earlier rain had stopped, water dripped down from trees still green under a blue umbrella. The drips tapped, plopped, staccato and slow harmonizing. Sam's claws scraped on pavement as her hind legs dragged due to dysplasia in her hips. As I stooped to go under some tree branches, hold them up for Jean, water dripped into my ear and my eyes met those of two black and white cats watching us from under the trees as we went past. Sam didn't notice, or didn't care, head down, intent on keeping going. A red plastic straw lay in the gutter. Roses, geraniums, pale blue hydrangeas moved through their season of light, and a couple of black poodles, ears flying, larked about together in a field. Gulls cried from somewhere hidden in heights of sky. Little yellow birds flitted among wet leaves, sang a brilliant intense moment and flew away. We were enclosed together in a wet morning, tuned into our own preoccupations, moving in our private tracks, circling, coming round again to a different bend.

On one drive, to Stanley Park, Jean began to sing quietly, "When I grow too old to dream...." then said, "My time is over, it's all done now, finished, nothing's left—time catches everything, where have I gone?" I remembered as a child hearing her sing that song, and others, Scottish folk songs, and popular ballads during the war years, "Look for the Silver Lining .... I'll be Seeing You," others I can't remember now, except one I will always think of as Jean's song, by Stephen Foster, "I dream of Jeannie with the light brown hair, born like a vapour on the soft summer air...." her voice, even then, never quite on tune; I hear it still.

Sam, our thirteen-year-old golden retriever, had a crisis while I was in France. She became too sick to remain at the kennel where she was boarded during my absence, where they let her wander around with them rather than keeping her penned, because she was old, quiet, and slow. She was brought home by my son to where friends and family could take turns caring for her until I returned. As August was ending, it did not look good. Fluid was collecting on her lungs, swelling her chest, her muzzle; she looked as though she'd gotten into a hive of bees. Her struggles for breath at night made me realize I couldn't let her go on suffering. Having the fluid drawn off her lungs was a temporary relief, but this became just as stressful for her. Her vet called to say the cells in the fluid she'd drawn off were not normal, some kind of cancer tumour blocked necessary drainage. I called a friend and asked if she would come and sit with me until I could find the courage to call the vet to come and give Sam the injection to release her. I wanted it done at home where she wouldn't be frightened, this gentle golden dog who trembled so hard at the vet's she left puddles of sweat behind her as though she'd peed all over the floor. All afternoon we sat on the front porch with Sam and fed her morsels of melon and cantaloupe, stroking her, until finally I was able to make the call. Two women arrived, the vet and her assistant, empathetic and efficient. Sam left as I looked into her eyes. The women carried her out wrapped in a pink blanket they brought with them. There were a lot of tears after Sam died, unusual for me, as I usually held tears back. It seemed Sam was bringing me back in touch with myself again, perhaps, in some ways, for the first time. There was a dream during that time, of walking on paths that curved, first through what seemed a forest that was silver as though covered in hoarfrost, then through mostly fields with weeds and bushes I could see over. I feel alone but there is someone with me. I can't see who it is. I needed to tell Jean why Sam was no longer with us on our walks and drives. When I did, she expressed sympathy, was quiet, something gently sad there, for me, I think; something left unsaid.

When I next came to take Jean for a drive, I found Kleenex everywhere, some wadded, some lying on the floor, and a washcloth and a pair of underwear in the pocket of her blouse. She was wearing two blouses. We drove, that day, again through those huge cedar trees in Stanley Park that seemed to have been there forever, followed the ocean's shore along English Bay, over Burrard Bridge to Kits Beach, and parked by a grassy slope of trees, the ocean beyond. We had the tea and muffins I had stopped to pick up along the way. Leaves, brown, dry, were drifting down; a sailboat with black sails out there on water the colour of pewter, wind in dry leaves a sound of the sea. When I brought Sam to this shore, she told me in her animal way that it was our last walk, as she sat looking around at everything, scanning the horizon, then looked at me, from over her shoulder, turned herself around with her back to it all, and did not look back. By the time we got to the car her strength was gone and I had to ask someone walking at the beach to help me get her back into the car.

Fall, 1992, brought me into the second year of my graduate program at UBC. My thesis would be a collection of poetic short fiction. I wanted to know more about my grandmother Jane, anything. I wrote a short story, a fiction, an act of imagination about her, my mother, my daughter, and myself; four generations of women, and titled it, "Emily Leaves the Garden." It became a liberation and a hunger to know more, that muted and buried selves could be written out of silence into their own stories. I had written away to Jean's birthplace, requesting information about Jean's family. I realized I had not thought of them as family of mine, that there was a sense in me of a dislocation. I wanted to know what restrained women from being themselves, and with each other, what had muted Jean, what was held in her memory, her body's cells; her story.

I hadn't been told that Jean was given the anti-psychotic loxapine, on two or three occasions while I was away in France, because, her records said, she was *aggressive, hitting other residents*. It was then prescribed to be used *as situations arise*. When I became aware of this, through a casual conversation with someone on staff, it was months later, fall 1992. I consulted with Jean's doctor and indicated my unwillingness for Jean to be given these drugs, and that I wished to be notified of any problems with her care immediately. In muting Jean, imposing "order" on what was perceived as her "disorder," there appeared to be no reflection on care that was appropriate for Jean, or that these drugs actually caused abnormal behaviours. In the meantime, the director of nursing told me: "Jean needs loxapine." Later it would become evident that not only loxapine but a whole range of anti-psychotics, not only had a damaging effect on Jean, but, as I would soon discover, were associated in medical literature with a range of physiologically, neurologically injurious effects, including paradoxical (reverse) and rebound effects (between doses and when withdrawn). Persons over sixty , the literature indicated, were at particular risk. The director of nursing then told me: "You need to come to terms with the fact that nothing you do will make any difference to Jean's memory." After this I had a dream. I was with Jean, showing her Portage Avenue in Winnipeg where we lived, Portage Avenue, the street where Jean worked, where she shopped for her clothes at Eaton's and the Bay, where she dreamed of being a "buyer for Eaton's," she told me in a rare moment. In the dream, Portage Avenue is derelict, the boulevards gone wild and there are no buildings left on either side of the street. I am looking at her wondering what her reaction will be.

The next day I asked Jean about the little village where we lived before I was five and we moved to Winnipeg. She tried to place it. I reminded her we went to Winnipeg. Jean, silent for a moment, asked, "Were you alone while I was working? Who looked after you?" I said that most of the time I was at school. I described where we lived. Jean sat down heavily on her bed, her face expressed felt pain, and a kind of a dry, harsh sob came out of her. She looked up at me. "Were they hard places for you, those places where we lived?" It was hard for both of us, I said, sitting down beside her on the bed. "Yes," she said slowly, shaking her head from side to side in what seemed anguish, grief. I accepted this unexpected acknowledgement as a gift. It was a dark time in her life. Jean lost her mother, a brother, a nephew, and her husband between when I was three and eleven; and from the time I was five, a war on, we lived in those two rooms with no running water on Osborne Street, with no one around to look after me when she was at work. My father, before his death, was only home some weekends for the duration of the war, away teaching young military recruits "the three R's," he told me once, when I'd asked, laughing as though he was apologizing. I put my arm around Jean.

The sepia photos I had framed and put up on a shelf, of Jean as a child, with her mother, and the school in the town where she grew up, I occasionally found face down, or turned towards the wall. "They leave you alone here," she said one day when we were having tea in her room. She meant it in a good way, reflecting her need for privacy. And later, near tears, talking about her mother, Jane, "such a kind, fine person, never hurt anyone...."

December, 1992, drew us into winter, holding another spring. Jean cried now, for her mother Jane, telling me again what a good person she was, "poor, very poor," she added. We talked about how Jean felt about her mother having such a hard life, always "doing for others," especially her father and brothers, the men who came to work or help out on the farm. Jean seemed to have good memories of her brothers. I remembered she'd once said to me, some years ago, randomly, it seemed at the time, that her father "drank," and had no idea then of what was contained in that word *drank*. It was of her mother Jean continued to speak, how Jane took her visiting, that they went to the garden together to pick vegetables. "She always found a way to get the things we needed, clothes and food, always farm stuff, nothing in the house...." Jean meant by this they had little, were "too poor." Once living in town, her mother "never went out, never did things for herself." As the tears ran down Jean's cheeks then, I felt her disappointment, her hurt at what had happened to her mother, and about how her mother would always make everything so nice and the men would come in and eat it all up. I told her daughters could get angry about the seeming inability of their mothers to change their lives. Jean agreed, nodded, "Yes," she said, "I was the only girl, they left me alone to do as I pleased. I didn't have chores like the others." Yet, a trapped life, her mother's and hers, although different; feeling some sense of my own life trapped in Jean, her unknown life, and was hungry for these fragments. I told her it was good to know these things, that I didn't know very much about her, or my grandmother. Jean said then, "I was a little inward over those years...." I remembered, once, over a cup of tea, some years before, Jean looking at me and saying, "It's a wonder anyone survives growing up." I thought she meant me.

New Year's Day, 1993, was Jean's eighty-ninth birthday. There was very little in her records as this year closed, an *irregular pulse, congested chest*. I had been given nitroglycerine pills to take on our outings. The pills remained unused. A small growth on Jean's chin worried me. It turned out to be what was referred to as *invasive, well-differentiated squamous cancer*. I had advised staff I would no longer be helping with bathing, feeling that when I was there assisting staff, too many people were on hand and created confusion, that by now the care staff, I thought, should be familiar with Jean. Some staff never had a problem, told me this. It was a matter of their approach. A note I found much later in her records regarding this indicated what I neither said nor implied, quoting me as saying the staff was to: *handle the bathing in our own way, even to use physical measures*. This was another of the skewed interpretations of my comments and responses that appeared in Jean's records, and no doubt also influenced what happened to Jean, particularly from this point on. Later I would take her bathing over on my own, without any problems, an unfamiliar intimacy. Jean's records at that point still indicated her physician was the one with whom we had severed all connections, rather than her new GP who had been acting as her doctor for the past ten months, since she became a resident here. By then I had a growing sense of something seriously wrong with communication in this facility, and that, again, I was the one who must hold it all together, if Jean was to be safe.

Spaces

Where does our sense of home lie? Home, belonging, do they mean the same thing? Was memory Jean's home now, all that she carried within her, memory splitting, shifting, slippery, bruising, uncovering ... stories winding, unwinding, the past alive? How we relate to that which is around us; locate ourselves, navigate, is it easily lost? Will we always be ourselves, no matter what? Late into January of this new year, 1993, I was not told what I found later, written in her records, of several episodes during the night or early evening: *threatening ... belligerent ... talking loudly and angrily ... very aggressive behaviour towards staff and residents ... violent... kicking at other residents, very agitated ... wanting everyone "out of her house."* I was told only that Jean had become "agitated." Concerned that the so-called anti-psychotics or anti-anxiety drugs might be used on her again, I met with her doctor, and also discovered Jean was offered several cups of coffee each day and there was no decaffeinated coffee available. After my requesting it, decaffeinated coffee was made available in the facility, and although it was written in Jean's records that this was all she was to have, changing staff never seemed aware of this. After my talk with Jean's doctor, his written orders for what nursing staff call her *aggression* are: food + TLC *(tender loving care)*.

Jean and I continued our walks when it wasn't raining, or the sidewalks slippery with frost. Or we would have decaf coffee or tea, and cookies, fruit that I often brought with me, things I knew she liked, have this in her room, when it wasn't good walking weather. Staff did not seem pleased that Jean did not go downstairs to the lounge for this. Facility staff consistently either ignored, or did not comprehend Jean's need for quiet and privacy and how her equanimity could be affected by their loss.

By Valentine's Day, Jean was leaning noticeably to the right side when she walked. She was talking about her life on the farm, " the poor, cold house." Her mother "worked very hard, worked her head off to feed and clothe them, to take care of things. Made do with little." She spoke hesitantly of her father, as she never had, as "he, him … we didn't like him very much … hard to understand, people didn't take to him, he wanted his own way of doing things, things done his way, didn't care about us, what you wore or had to eat—lazy, you had to watch for hardness, kicks, my brothers all left in high school to work and make enough money, didn't get a chance to make something of themselves…" Jean was crying, her chin trembling, and saying how good her mother was to them, kind, that her father "couldn't care less." I asked if he was mean to her. She didn't respond, silent, until I mentioned an older cousin who was mean to me when I spent a few weeks time on their farm as a child, one summer, and then Jean said, "Just like my father, same thing." Jean said then she "spent a lot of time alone," her mother "took care of her but had no time to spend with her," that she had "stayed out of her father's way." Her brothers all left, "not a good growing up—always uneasy." Jean said then, "You know, a young child feels things, is open to whether people are treated fairly, kindly, or are given a kick. It wasn't a good growing up. I shouldn't complain." Of her brother whose son had harassed me on their farm, something I had never told Jean, she said, "I always felt I shouldn't say it because he was my brother, but I didn't like him very much. He was mean." Then she told me she used to lie out in the grass on the farm when there was no one to talk to, or climb trees … "just the chickens … nobody." She mentioned a row of dead snakes her brothers hung along the fence. It was better when they moved into town, "more money, more jobs." Her mother was "fun, laughed a lot, not at people," she added quickly, said she "liked to be at the table with her mother, but she wanted to get away, up and up and up, to university, to have money for herself and clothes." I told her then I thought it was important to say these things. She nodded, seemed to know how I meant it. Two days later there was a note in Jean's file: *further leaning to the right, possible TIA, aggression.* The TIA refers to a transient ischemic attack—a mini-stroke. A possible clot, thrown off by an irregular heartbeat, that lodges in the brain. As winter slipped into spring, Jean one day made a very quick reference to death, looked over at me in a covert way. Jean always asked if I was alright, was everybody alright? She listened and nodded anytime I gave her news of her grandchildren. How are they? She smiled.

Spring, 1993, and this note appeared in her records: *agitated +++ ie. demanding staff to tell her where her mother is, why she can't remember things etc. reassurance given +++ asking all the residents to leave her house, attempted to hit a fellow resident....* There is no information noted regarding what exactly happened or what the circumstances were. Tracking pieces of voice to spaces in the heart ... fear below, soundings, wounds held in cells of memory, lifetime of unbound grief. I felt it too, this welling up of risk, head harnessed to heart. Jean leading the way now, taking us home. Spring birds returned to my feeder; feelings of enjoyment, comfort so remote and hard to come by had become a distraction to going on with getting things done, my graduate work, watching over Jean. When I brought in bedding plants to plant in Jean's window garden again this spring, the women who always seemed to be sitting by the nursing station, do they ever get to go outside, I wondered, watched me like birds, with a look in their eye, a small light from embers of hunger. I walked over and held the boxes out to them ... marigolds, zinnias, petunias, geraniums ... their hands reaching, touching petals, my heart.

Jean was speaking again of her father, talking carefully, telling me she "would have wanted a different father if she had it to do over again. He didn't care what we did, whether we got an education ... didn't provide for his family ... we didn't have what other people had." Then I heard her say, "things I couldn't tell anybody that still make me cry, that hurt," and that "moving into town away from the farm seemed like joining the world." She said she "didn't play games with others my age, afraid of getting hurt, played by myself out on the farm," mentioned the trees, animals, and always the garden, and about how her mother "didn't get anything for all her work, left without money when he died.

... men ... how they treat women." She said she "wouldn't let men, husbands do that to me...." She did not mention my father. I told her what I did know of him, my father, which was very little. I wanted to know more, but she became silent.

Jean's records rarely contained any indication or reference to causes for what was indicated as "episodes of her behaviour," causes external to Jean, such as environmental conditions, staff behaviour and inappropriate approaches to Jean, or her state of health, interrupted sleep, etc., to say nothing of the confusion and frustration of trying to orient herself, and deal with short-term memory loss. Running through all her records were subjective reactions to Jean, and blaming. There was anticipation of behaviour commensurate with how she had been labelled. No appreciation for who she was and what she was going through was ever noted. She was presented as a problem to be managed through suppression by drugging. The GP, who had been her doctor since entering this care facility, had been respectful, conversational, and even playful with Jean. I had never seen any difficulty between them, rather a pleasant friendly rapport, as though he was a younger brother. He seemed aware of Jean the person; tried to encourage staff to provide food during the evening and night if she needed it, writing orders in her records for TLC, and a walking program. However, his compliance with the facility's staff requests that Jean be given the anti-psychotic loxapine, first of all, occasionally, for what staff referred to in her records as *striking out,* without description of what this meant, or documentation of the circumstances, was disturbing to me. But this was only the beginning. By May 1993, her records indicated: *Very resistant to a.m. bath. Food and* TLC *not effective, refusing to have hair washed..* Two days later loxapine was ordered and by May 25, her doctor wrote in her records: *Has required loxapine twice. No report of immediate effect.* In fact this facility's records indicated, and would continue to demonstrate that Jean became more agitated in the aftermath of these doses of loxapine. Just what knowledge this physician had regarding these brain-disabling drugs, and their propensity to cause psychosis, muscle pain, and rigidity, particularly in an older person, Jean now eighty-nine, and their rebound effects when withdrawn, was not clear to me. What I could see was that he allowed this drug to be given to Jean intermittently on the word of care staff. Later I would be browbeaten, threatened with Jean's removal from this facility and told by staff that it was likely "no one else will take her." Again the threat of Riverview Mental Hospital, if I did not allow Jean to be drugged.

By the end of May, I managed to convince Jean's doctor to discontinue loxapine. Spring, a year ago, Jean was also given loxapine, then I was leaving for France. Spring when I left home for my first job in Toronto, spring when Jean took me and left on the train to Winnipeg, from our small village home in Manitoba, spring when she married my father... spring when her breast was removed and her heart went wild. Mother's Day in May. There were no more entries of any kind on Jean's file after the loxapine was discontinued, until summer, when her doctor wrote: *puzzles over reading material, says letters are <u>clear</u> but can't read well ... strikes out if <u>rushed</u> cooperative when <u>flattered</u> steady intellectual decline consistent w. Alzheimers with background of strokes ... fibrillation.* It was disappointing to know, when reading this in 1995, that her doctor, who did not see Jean all that often, had more than likely been repeating staff attitudes in these notes in Jean's records, and as a result, compounded an attitude toward Jean that would continue to set her up as unmanageable and in need of medication. The choice of the word *flattered* was particularly lacking in respect for Jean. Why not a word that reflected genuine caring, like complimented, or treated with compassion, interest, etc.? A few weeks later, August by then, her doctor gave Jean a more complete yearly exam in her room, in my presence. This time he recorded a more personal impression of Jean which questioned his former notation of a process of mental deterioration, as in organic brain disease: *Reads normal print with glasses but has trouble following a sentence-slow. Enjoys a silly sentence and can compensate for memory and concentration by joking* .... He noted her pulse was irregular. Had her walk a straight line with her eyes closed, which she did, and he commented: *In better physical shape than most here. Multi-infarct on background of ? Alzheimers. Cheerful; likes it here. Refuses mammogram. Had refused anti-coagulation in past....* On this closer contact with Jean, without the presence of facility staff, her doctor's focus returned to multi-infarct ischemic episodes as the source of her short-term memory and orientation problems, questioning his previous suggestion of organic brain disease. He wanted to start Jean on the anti-coagulation medication coumarin, but I did not feel I could make that choice for her, not only because Jean had refused it, but because, with Jean's history of duodenal bleeding, should she begin to bleed internally there would be a time lag, because of the blood thinner present in her system, before the haemorrhaging could be stopped. I was requested to take Jean for a mammogram of her right breast, which was negative, and to bring her to her doctor's office, where he attempted to obtain a pap smear. After beginning the procedure, he frowned, muttered something about not trying further. I was therefore surprised and disappointed to see in Jean's records his note: *pt.* (patient) *refused further exam.* Jean did not refuse anything, she was quite cooperative and quiet. I was there. Once again the problem was shifted onto Jean, who couldn't argue, wouldn't be believed, in records unavailable to me for scrutiny at that time.

Jean's records from that time also revealed what was not communicated to me then, that the digoxin level in Jean's blood had been checked because of missed dosages of digoxin, which apparently, according to what was termed *an incident report,* Jean had refused. Although her blood level of digoxin, which subsequently measured at 0.5nmol/L, was much less than what is considered a toxic level, and markedly less than the level of 1.8nmol/L considered in a toxic range that her blood test had indicated, prior to entering the care facility, when she was under the care of her former GP, and that, at the time of this much lower digoxin level, there were no heart *palpitations* and her recorded heart rate *more normal* than in the past, yet no connection was made between her lower blood level reading of digoxin and the improved rate and stability of Jean's heart. An EKG was ordered, which Jean refused and it was noted in her record that *she may have to be sedated.*

Fear the wall; fear and risk, hand in glove, a door in the wall to let the body know what it already knows, finding lost voice, finding the heart. The rational mind is where the panic lies, in an illusion of "control." A letter arrived from the town where Jean was born, where her mother Jane lived and survived, outliving her husband by another seventeen years. Information, in response to my request, came as xeroxed accounts of my grandfather's prizes for growing wheat, his membership in various farming associations, his ten sons, their war service, and a daughter Jean. Jane was not mentioned by name, she simply appeared as "wife of" my grandfather. She had gone missing. Why? Did I really want this, if family history it was, this weight and context? I wanted my own life as mine. Is this what Jean wanted for herself, and perhaps for me, keeping it from me, getting away from it all, the sadness, the hardness? I was looking for a language for the spaces that had none, finding lost voices, feeling where the fear lay. Over the summer I had developed what a doctor referred to as an allergic laryngo-tracheitis inflammation. It was difficult to swallow, my throat was sore, and it hurt to speak.

"I always like Fran," Jean said to me one day, as summer came to an end. We were driving through Stanley Park. Clouds had come, mist through the mountain passes, inlets, rain in the distance, like smoke, light shining through it—a double rainbow. Cool, then warm, hot, cool again, boats, distant voices, silent sails go by. Remembering arbutus trees. They twist and lean, keeping their leaves, shedding orange strips of their skin and their red berries down onto slippery shale slanting into clear water, summer slipping into fall. Later, while walking, Jean said, "I'm falling." She smiled. She was leaning to the right, her body twisting, speech a little mixed. Possibly transient ischemic episodes, her doctor suggested, and if not the blood thinner coumarin, then he wanted to prescribe daily Aspirin. I was concerned about her bleeding. Children's Aspirin should be okay, he thought.

Jean's records at this time state: *resistance to bathing and having her hair washed continues,* but no details were supplied. Some staff continued to tell me they had no problem with Jean in this regard, others had the wisdom to let the situation go and try again later. Those who had problems referred to her as *resistant and hostile.* There had been many suggestions on my part regarding bathing. How closely they were followed, if at all, I did not know. I reminded staff again about Jean's need to feel in control and suggested that, for hair washing, she be given a dry cloth to hold over her eyes to protect them. I had begun to suspect there was some kind of pain in her neck and made staff aware of this and, when I learned male nurses were assisting with personal care, on instinct, I requested that only female care staff assist Jean. It seemed to me that if Jean was being put into situations where she was not helped to feel she had some choice, or control, and with no way to remove herself, this was more than likely to bring on stress and some form of resistance that might not be at all specific, expressed in the form of a generalized agitation, especially when articulating was difficult or, as it often is under stress, impossible. To this point, I believed I had been viewed as *cooperative and supportive of staff,* as the records stated at one point. The nursing staff did not appear to me to appreciate too many questions or my questioning of medications. I did not receive much information from staff regarding Jean. My queries, often when I came in to be with her, were usually met with "she's fine" or "she's been agitated," if I queried further. I had, since Jean entered this facility, resisted her being given any kind of behaviour-modifying drug. It was her records, which I obtained after her death, that left so many unanswered questions regarding this facility's ability to administer and deliver care that was safe for Jean and according to her need.

A dream at this time: I am holding the hand of a child with no feet, all head, no ground; panic feels like energy with no place to go. I had just turned in my thesis collection of "poetic fiction" half a year late, having received an extension to complete it by that fall. It was returned to me with directions to excise all of the internal dialogue of the women in my stories, the fears and uncertainties, the gaps, silences, the questions, which, it was suggested to me, crippled the narrative line. But these, to me, were the narrative, the streaming of fragments, pieces of voice, like water, light; their stories, the heart. Their own internal logic would be excised from them. A low and angry point. I did not want the women in my stories to be lost, and decided I would not do the excising requested. I did not want Jean excised either, or Jane, or myself. Social memory can be obscured by misleading language. I wanted to retrieve, reclaim stories that had been silenced, not revise them into further silence, and wrote a letter to that effect. My thesis was then accepted as it was.

Out of Time

The inconsistency, or absence, of effective communications between various levels and areas of facility staff and between these and myself became particularly and critically evident in the fall of 1993. Soon after Jean was given 80 mg of children's Aspirin daily, she had a haemorrhaging nosebleed during the night and was taken by ambulance to an emergency ward. Described in facility records as *aggressive and resistant to anyone touching her nose or taking her blood pressure*, yet she was also described in these notes as *cooperative with paramedics*. I telephoned at 3:00 a.m after she was taken to emergency, and told not to go to the emergency ward because Jean would be back at the facility shortly. I asked them to call me when she was expected back and then I called the emergency ward and was told the same thing: "No point in coming down, she could be gone again by the time you get here." I continued to call the emergency, was told Jean was "just fine, right here by the nursing station." I regretted deeply not following my instincts to be with her. What they did not tell me was that Jean had been strapped to a gurney, no doubt frightened, confused, and experiencing difficulty breathing because of the bleeding. At some point she was drugged. She was returned to her room at the care facility and did not regain full consciousness until late into the following day, visibly shaken as she told me quietly, with something broken in her voice, that she was yelled at and told to "shut up." Jean's fragility, alone in an emergency ward. I should have gone anyway, no matter what I was told. It was an abuse of her rights to be treated as she was, and then drugged to control the resulting agitation so reasonable in the circumstances. From this point on, I felt Jean's mental, emotional and physical being, her rights as a person, coming under more overt threat, as well as my ability to protect her.

In the next three weeks, Jean showed signs of being ill, congestion in her chest, coughing, swollen ankles, confusion not inconsistent with illness-associated delirium, particularly in someone of her age. The nurse refused to call her doctor, telling me "unless there is an emergency Jean will be seen on his next visit to the facility," which, she told me, might be a couple of weeks. When I told her this wouldn't do, Jean needed to be seen immediately, she became hostile. I insisted the doctor be called. This nurse was very angry. I didn't know whether she didn't believe that Jean was sick, or just didn't want to call in the doctor. I became ill with flu and could not go in to be with Jean for some days and repeated my request by telephone. Her signs of illness had begun to appear in early October and it was late October before she was finally seen by her doctor and diagnosed with bronchitis. She was then given antibiotics, after which her edema cleared. She told me, "I want to go home now, to my mother." I thought then about it being the anniversary of my father's, her husband's, death. It was during this period when she was ill, and unknown to me, that incident reports were being filed and placed in her records regarding her "behaviour," but there was no reference at all in these reports to her being ill. Instead they state: *unprovoked verbal aggression and violent behaviour ... resistant to care, difficult to manage in all aspects of care.*

One nurse, an RN, was responsible for all these reports and for initiating at this time, without my knowledge, Jean's reassessment by Long Term Care for removal from this care facility. One of her reports described *aggressive & potential violet* (violent) *behaviour on approach, awake all night, short period of noisiness—banging on cupboard door with handle of a brush for x 10 mins, Won't listen to reasoning, irritable confused, irrational and no insight. Staff members ignored her to let her calm down.* This nurse did not indicate anywhere in her reports that Jean was ill, nor that staff had suddenly and without warning to Jean or myself, locked her cupboard door so she couldn't have access to her clothing; their reasoning for this, to prevent her from mixing clothing she'd worn with what was clean. Nothing in any of this RN's reports was communicated to me. Jean's *reassessment* to be moved from this facility took place without my knowledge. In early November, I received a phone call from someone I did not know, not connected with the facility, but who liaised with the care facility and Long Term Care, informing me Jean was being removed from the facility and that I "should be looking at some secure facilities and put her on a wait-list." Riverview Mental Hospital was mentioned to me. I was in shock. Not a word had been said to me that there was even a problem. Collecting my thoughts somewhat, I asked what the basis was for removing Jean from her home, and was told she was "unmanageable," based on what was written in Jean's records by that one RN, and what had been indicated verbally by what were referred to as "unidentified staff members." I was then referred to the director of care for this facility, if I wanted more information.

The director of care did not have the incident reports. It wasn't clear she had ever even seen them. I requested them, and at a subsequent meeting she read the reports generated by the RN, which made no mention of Jean's illness over the period of those reports or of any other stressors such as environmental factors, including staff shortages, overwork or lack of training and insight into care regarding a person in Jean's condition. As I pointed this out and discussed Jean's ill health at the time, the director acknowledged another look at Jean's situation was in order. At this point, mid-November, the facility's director of nursing and director of admissions had both resigned, and the present director of care, with whom I was speaking, was carrying both these workloads in addition to her own. She told me, then, that in several weeks, by January, 1994, she too would be gone, having already given in her resignation. It became difficult to impossible to find consistent lines of communication in order to deal with Jean's ongoing situation and it was now obvious that there were problems in employee relations at this facility, stressors that not only interfered with Jean's care according to her individual needs, but also appeared to be generating hostility and resentment toward her. There were individual care givers who made a point of telling me they did not have problems with Jean and others who told me she was "sometimes agitated, but nothing we can't handle."

By mid-November I was told Jean was "on trial," her "behaviour" would be monitored for the next month. There were no further "incidents" after she was treated for bronchitis. Jean's doctor wrote in her records at this time: *I do not favour the use of anti-psychotics in this pt.* As a result of discussions I had with him and the facility's director, staff were advised to be more aware of Jean's fatigue, provide nourishment between meals and overnight, use a quiet approach and recognize Jean wished to be on her own in her room and walked the halls as a natural physical activity. Staff did not seem to be aware that I was coming in several times a week to help Jean with her clothing changes, and that I had begun assisting Jean with her showering/hair washing once a week on my own, with no staff present. There were never any problems at any time between us as I assisted her with these, nor at any other time. I would spend the afternoon in her room, drying her hair, putting it into rollers, and then bring her a cup of decaf coffee or tea and cookies or a muffin, some fruit. A note that I was coming in to assist her with bathing had been placed in her care records, yet still I would find that prior to, or after, my coming and helping her to shower, staff would approach Jean to do the same. I reminded them of this lack of communication, but by December nursing staff were talking of drugging Jean if she would not "cooperate" with being bathed.

December 14, under pressure from the facility, her doctor ordered a *Buspar trial for anxious/paranoid behaviour during bathing, 5mg. 3x/ day.* A so-called anti-anxiety drug. This was the dosage pharmaceutical literature indicates as an introductory dose for those under sixty. Jean would be ninety in eighteen days. Some of the side and adverse effects listed for this drug were: *headache, nausea, vomiting, drowsiness, insomnia, excitability, confusion, anger/hostility, hallucinations, cardio-vascular effects, respiratory effects.* Other studies indicated a syndrome of restlessness appearing shortly after initial use of this drug and a benzodiazapene-type withdrawal or rebound effect that could occur upon sudden withdrawal of this drug, or even between doses. After discontinuation, symptoms observed include: *anxiety, insomnia, restlessness, agitation, irritability, muscle tension, psychosis, seizures, persistent tinnitus, confusion, paranoid delusions, hallucinations.* The facility referred to this as "medication for Jean's unpredictable aggression." Pressure came at me as well, to agree to this drugging, the shadow of Riverview Mental Hospital always hovering nearby. There seemed little I could do but indicate my disagreement.

By New Year's Day, Jean's ninetieth birthday, she had been given the drug Buspar, involuntarily, since mid-December. Both her grandsons, in Vancouver for Christmas, came with me to celebrate. We brought flowers, her favourite chocolate cake. I wasn't sure, but she seemed disappointed with the silk blouse and the skirt when she unwrapped them, so difficult, always, to choose for her. We took photos, Jean sitting with her grandsons, smiling, gentle, looking directly at the camera, alert. The following night, January 2, Jean was reported as *up the whole night, but quiet, seemed disoriented and agitated, with irregular pulse.*

Jean began to list more noticeably and consistently to the right over the next few weeks. On January 10, based on what facility staff told him, Jean's doctor noted: *Buspar is controlling her aggression well.* The next day Jean was reported *aggressive, gesture to hit staff, swearing and incoherent of speech, no insight into her behaviour, awake most of the night.* As they continued giving her BuSpar, her records indicated intermittent and continuing episodes of the above occurred through January, as well as sleeplessness. When we went for walks, Jean had become short of breath and had developed a shuffle. At the end of January, despite my coming in to assist Jean with showering every week, two or three staff decided to use force to bathe her. Her hands were solid purple from bruising, as a result of being held down. When I queried this, the nurse on duty described their *fight* with Jean with a gleam in her eye something akin to triumph of accomplishment, and told me that the bruising "is normal." I felt an attempt to co-opt me into making Jean the cause of her own abuse.

On January 25, 1994, a care conference about Jean was reported in her records, written by the same nurse who initiated the threat of Jean's removal from this facility Her report for this conference included examples of highly subjective, selective, and questionable comments and opinions, and made no attempt to place Jean's actions in the context of the drug BuSpar and its effects on her; for example: *impossible to do any care because of extreme verbal and physical aggression ... changes clothes only after weekly bath.* I assisted Jean to change frequently when I came in, but did not press the matter when other things seemed more important; had once, jokingly, said to care staff that I guessed as long as she wasn't running naked through the halls, having a few extra skirts on was nothing to worry about. No one seemed particularly amused. This nurse's report continued ... *daughter still helps with bath but resident still dislikes it* (how would this nurse know? There was never a problem between Jean and myself) ... *sleeps and dresses in whatever she feels like* (this spoken by a professional nurse about someone with a short-term memory problem) ... *sarcastic and unreasonable—verbally and physically aggressive—many incidents of hitting staff and other* ... *residents* ... *nosebleed in October 93 had to be packed at* ....(the name of the hospital was incorrect) ... *ankle edema treated with digoxin—refused elastic stockings* (fact: the edema cleared up on its own after antibiotics were given to her for her bronchitis; no elastic stockings were ever offered). This nurse seemed somewhat confused regarding the purpose of the digoxin. Her report finished: ... *extreme aggression treated with Buspar* ... *wanders in the halls before supper* ... *sometimes wanders halls after supper* ... *usually calm* (calms) *down after being ignored by staff.*

In another report placed in Jean's file, this nurse used the term paranoiac with reference to Jean. Of the many nurses I dealt with, some of whom I knew by name, I did not remember her, or if I did have contact with her, I did not know her by name. I discovered these incomplete, inaccurate, and biased records about Jean long after they had done their damage, after Jean's death, when all I could do was request an investigation of this facility and make a formal complaint regarding this individual RN. She was "talked to," nothing placed on her personnel record, because, the Registered Nurses Association of BC, suggested, "the problem is systemic."

A summary of this conference by the facility's administrator, who was filling in for the now resigned director of care suggested, for the first and only time, that approaches taken by staff might be a factor in what was seen as Jean's "outbursts." The facility's records showed evidence of what was never connected by the facility, that as Jean remained on BuSpar, insomnia and agitation resulted, continued, and increased. She was described as *becoming aggressive towards other residents who come too close* and that sometimes she *did not sleep all night.* This was not communicated to me at that time. Instead, on February 5, the same nurse who informed me of the successful physical battle to bathe Jean entered Jean's room while I was with her and said loudly, in front of Jean, and smiling, that the BuSpar was "not working," and the dose had been doubled to 10 mg 3x/day. Her manner appeared to me to be adversarial, triumphant. Early the next morning Jean was reported: *very aggressive and leaning to the side and backward.* I could see more and more of these effects, whenever we walked together, since she had been exposed to the drug BuSpar, a listing to one side or the other, shuffling, and a leaning, sometimes backwards, sometimes forward, as though she was unable to stop herself. Aggression was something I never saw when I was with Jean. Four days later Jean's records noted: *due to her aggressive and unpredictable behaviour meals will be in a segregated area.* I was not told this. February 8, a more sympathetic nurse told me that, "someone in the house who's not supposed to be" always seemed to be the issue in Jean's "agitated episodes." Side and adverse effects associated with BuSpar, and rebound effects between doses, did include hallucinations, respiratory effects, and paranoid delusions. I had gone to search the literature when Jean was first given this drug. No connection was, or would be, made to how Jean was being affected.

Jean didn't seem to remember my birth, when I asked her. I had come to be with her in the evening to see if this would help calm her for the night. "Nothing went wrong with any of them," was all she said. I didn't know where she was in her memory, just then, wondered if she had been thinking of her mother and all those births. She did speak of Jane this night, and of the men who "demanded work of her—all the dirty work, expected it from women," her mother didn't ask her to do any work, or to help her. Her brothers used to tell her to help her mother more. I asked if her brothers helped her mother and Jean gave me an emphatic "yes." In what language do the fragments come together? Jean, with some inner dignity, remained intact. The child, the hungry child, was always me, waiting, holding on for what was yet to come, a filling of the emptiness, a story of this woman called mother not yet told. Will there ever be enough story? Driven by the fear of losing what I have not had, the knowledge of this woman, my mother who cannot not exist; that I will not know who I am if the one who births me remains a stranger, or leaves.

February 15, 1994, Jean's records reported she was *walking unsteadily, crying and upset for an hour* and three days later, *leaning heavily to her left.* She had an episode of vomiting before breakfast. At this point I was notified, and requested that she be seen by her doctor, who suggested she had a viral infection. I discussed with him the likelihood of toxicity from the BuSpar, becoming more obvious as the dosage of this drug was increased. Four days later I came in to find Jean, approximately twenty minutes after having been given a dose of BuSpar, in full view of staff at the nursing station, by the elevators, doubled over, crying, unable to walk, confused and slurred of speech. No one appeared to notice, and I had to ask someone from the nursing station to come over and assist me take her to her room, knew it was likely they had been ignoring her. Nursing staff appeared unwilling to relate any of these symptoms to BuSpar or even to acknowledge to me they had just given it to Jean twenty minutes earlier. I notified her doctor that the drug was clearly having an adverse affect on Jean and requested, due to the serious rebound effects associated with this drug, that it be gradually reduced and withdrawn. In spite of this, it was discontinued immediately, which is contraindicated in pharmacological literature.

A few days later Jean told me she was "glad when I come." I began telling her about me, my life, gradually describing what I remembered of our life together, my growing up, and my father, I said his name, that he died, and he was her husband. She remembered, and cried, saying, "I couldn't cry before, just couldn't let it out, I had to go on." I sat beside her, put my arm around her, moved to tears comforting her and being comforted in some way by this long-lost grieving we never did together. Jean cried again about my being alone and I told her, yes, it was lonely. She too was a lonely child, and her childhood mixed and flowed with mine and both lonely children seemed to be there. I tried to comfort her, tell her that when she wasn't working she was always there, evenings, Sundays. Memories stirred, good ones, listening to Lux radio theatre on Monday nights while Jean did the ironing, she washed clothes on Sunday, when the smell of her oven baked beans, rice pudding, and jam pie filled our two rooms.... Jean had told me that Jane had made soup for her, and rice pudding. I was left wondering what had been misremembered, how I'd assembled the fragments according to need, perception. Now memory's kaleidoscope was shifting, fragments coming together another way, a different story. Something resolved here, something healed in the fracturing ... I cut her nails, touching the unfamiliar softness of her skin, its purple veins miniature trees, limbs entwined, knotted; skin scales flaking from around the nails. I rubbed them with rose and glycerine cream, drift of rose petals across the room ... fragrance, combed her hair, surprisingly red when wet, drying to soft silver. Her eyes could become like those of a startled animal in the forest, when voices came on over the intercom out in the hallway, along with her immediate self-conscious embarrassment, aware of her reaction. Was there a frightened child there, moving through layers, my grandmother Jane, her mother, in that buggy, Jean with her, what bearings, did the horse know the way? The child must stay in the garden, must not know what she knows. I wanted more slipping out of silence on a long journey to here, shape of tracks, Jean between the lines, in the spaces between the rows of Jane's garden. Jean holding her space close to her skin. Silent in this intimacy thrust upon us; lost bodies wandering the heart's mind now, the mind's heart, its surprising spaciousness.

Spring was returning on March winds. I had a dream. I am a young adult moving around from place to place looking for someone. There is an old woman who lives at the end of a large auditorium or hall. She looks like Jean. She has an easel up and is painting on a white background, a line drawing of a cat, and another of a cat on a chair in front of a fireplace. There is a fire lit there. The dream ends with two older women hugging and laughing and they seem to be celebrating.

After a visit to Jean, her doctor recorded: *cheerful, does heel-toe walk with excellent balance and is better off Buspar, aggression best managed behaviourally.* Nursing records had continued to indicate BuSpar withdrawal symptoms (without acknowledging them as such), that Jean was *agitated*, experiencing more *episodes of leaning to one side or backwards, of crying and confusion.* When we walked together, these listings to the side, backwards, and her shuffling and racing forward were more and more obvious, along with increasing shortness of breath. By the end of March nursing records described Jean as: *verbally aggressive, verbally abusive, angry facial expression, argumentative, walking around with a coat hangar* (hanger) *waving it in a threatening manner.* By then I had received word from the Canada Council that I would receive a grant that I had applied for after completing my MFA last fall. It would fund a two-month trip to explore family history in Edinburgh, London, parts of Ontario, and Manitoba, and a further nine months of writing the first draft of a novel exploring generations of women, their absence from history, and what is passed on from their silences and absences. It would become a restored narrative, at its core, my journey with Jean, which became its skeleton, the spine that nourished every cell, that grew a tree from its roots, green, and breathing memory, generations flowing back and forth as a daughter, in the novel she is Lily, tells her dying mother and herself, and the reader, stories, so they will know their lives. I was

scheduled to leave in June. I wanted to tell Jean, arrived at the facility
to find staff ready to spray her room with a can of Raid and remove
all of Jean's clothing to be sterilized. Their intention was to completely
coat her skin with insecticidal permethrin, which would be left on for
twelve to fourteen hours as a prophylactic against scabies, ordered by
her doctor, because a nurse had reported she had seen some scratch
marks on Jean's upper back. Nursing records stated: *resident has rash
and scratch marks all over back.* I did not know if Jean's doctor had
actually come in to examine her, or had given the order for Jean to
be treated for scabies based on a phone call from staff, who were not
happy with my insistence that they wait until I obtained an emergency
appointment with a skin specialist, who found what he called "a
few scratch marks," which he attributed to dry skin and suggested a
moisturizer.

Helping Jean out of my car to attend her appointment with the skin
specialist, I took her full weight as she stumbled on the curb, which
wrenched the scar tissue from spinal surgery in my lower back, done
some years before. This scar tissue inflammation had happened once
before, incapacitating me for a lengthy period of time. Scar tissue is
like old shoe leather, a specialist had told me then, and the process of
softening it at that time was what took so long, well into my return to
university classes when my choice of courses depended on how long I
could sit at one time. Once these current spasms began, I was unable to
come in to visit Jean and take care of her, until acupuncture treatments
at home eased the spasms and I could move again, amazed that I could,
that acupuncture could bring such immediate relief, not only from pain
but also from my fear of being immobilized for a long time. During
this time, when I couldn't come in to be with Jean, nurses wrote in her
records that she appeared *at nursing station yelling and threatening
staff—waving a comb around. Ignored resident and in about an hour
settled and went to room. Refused to go to breakfast.* Just what the
nature is of this threat these young women at the nursing station saw
from a woman of ninety waving her comb around and yelling is not
made clear. There appeared in her records this repeated procedure of
staff to *ignore* Jean, let her take responsibility for the effects of their
drugging, and to see her as *threatening, violent and aggressive.* What
Jean's doctor found, when he was in direct contact with her, appeared
to contradict what he was told by the nursing staff and what they wrote
in her records. Where was safety for Jean? I was with Jean in her room,

watching dancers on television, one evening, when Jean looked at me, said, "Why am I here?" I took it as a measure of her despair, had no answer.

I needed to buy new shoes for Jean. A sign over the shoe display said, *Spirit, for women on the go*. Soft, supple, black, I picked these, in Jean's size, long and very narrow, brought them to her in a box. "What are these?" She had the box open, ran her fingers over the shoes. I suggested she should try them on to see if they fit. "Yes," she said, "soft aren't they ... were they a good price?" Yes, a really good price, I told her, undid the laces, laid them by her feet. She put them on and walked around her bed, said they were "fine," would last "all the way to winter." We walked out into the hallway. She left my arm, I could feel her go, with no hint of listing or shuffling, stepping, turning along the hall, in a gentle, delicate dance into the sunroom, threading tables and chairs, turned to me, her hands held out, open, palms up. She smiled, laughed. There were no words, words would erase, as they do with a dream that is too close, yet distant and disappearing, so near a mirage, clear as light; green as a tree.

By mid-April the facility viewed Jean's *behaviour as unacceptable*. A social worker, based on what she read in these records and comments by some staff, suggested a psychiatric referral. Jean's doctor was once again under pressure, this time to give Jean risperidone, described in pharmacological literature as a recently marketed (1994), atypical neuroleptic, with a particular tendency to produce adverse stimulant effects, including insomnia, agitation, and anxiety that may also account for risperidone-induced rage attacks, as well as headaches and hypotension, among others, and that previously diagnosed breast cancer may be activated by use of this drug. I was told that *if early results were not forthcoming*, Jean would be referred for a psychiatric consult. There was no mention in Jean's records at this point of the existence at the facility of a major environmental stressor over this period of April and May, which was the beginning of extensive renovations to the facility. This, when there also existed large gaps in essential staff positions, three as yet unfilled positions, that of director of care, director of nursing, and director of admissions. The acting director of care, formerly a senior on-line nurse, appeared to be attempting to fulfil all these responsibilities, as well as plan and oversee renovations which had begun in the area of the nursing station and adjacent to Jean's room, all producing noise, dust, fumes, and distress.

Workmen were active every day, often working around residents who were not ambulatory and seated in recliners by the nursing station. On one occasion I saw a worker throwing pieces of old drywall into a wheelbarrow, practically over the lap of an elderly resident. There was dust everywhere. No one at the nursing station seemed to even notice, let alone make a move to extricate these residents from the situation.

On May 4, 1994, I was called into a meeting with a social worker, the acting director of care, who was the liaison between the facility and Long Term Care, and Jean's doctor. I was told at this meeting that Jean "cannot be placed anywhere until her aggression is controlled and that she would now be on risperidone for her aggression." Jean's doctor, as we left the meeting, told me it was "out of his hands." In whose hands was it? Where does the responsibility and accountability lie? Who had final authority to drug Jean with this dangerous neuroleptic risperidone? These nurses and facility administrators had no training in neuroleptic pharmacology. Jean's doctor had demonstrated to me a lack in his understanding of anti-psychotics and their effects. This is a government-subsidized facility. On what basis does a government bureaucracy provide authority to medicate someone against their will without there being recourse to assessments as to the appropriateness of such action from outside this facility? I had no answers, and didn't know where to go to find them, if such existed. I felt fully occupied just trying to keep Jean as safe as I could. And so, on May 4, 1994, at ninety, Jean was given the anti-psychotic risperidone, which has also been implicated in the activation of breast cancer.

Staff had seemed happy enough for me to assist in Jean's care, as long as I didn't question how things were done, or question treatment, as long as I did not suggest she had a right not to be medicated and to be treated according to her needs. The shift in their attitude towards me as uncooperative remained covert but, I believe, became a threat to Jean. A careful politeness gave an impression they were involving me, but they were not listening as I urged consideration of other factors affecting Jean, the impact of drugs on her body and of delirium, documented in medical literature as caused by any number of factors: dehydration, infection, low blood oxygen, inadequate cardiac output, drugs, as well as sleep deprivation or an acute sense of loss of control, such as when medicated without consent, and can cause severe disorientation in time and place. Described as a "state of mental confusion in which an individual fails to remember what has been happening or understand events, and can suffer increased anxiety, physical restlessness, and sudden swings of mood, brought on by illness and/or disturbances of body chemistry, commonly precipitated by drugs, and if the underlying cause is not treated, can result in the sufferer experiencing the perception, for example, of nurses as threatening, and becoming panicked and agitated. These symptoms are usually worse at night."

While on risperidone Jean was described in her records: *withdrawing more and breaking out at others more ... awake all night, in and out of her room but quiet ... restless, has not been sleeping last three nights ... wandered from facility, brought back, tired, resting in her room....* After this, her doctor discontinued risperidone due to what he referred to in her records as *side effects.* Again he ignored the adverse rebound effects documented in the literature from sudden withdrawal of these neuroleptics. Within three days of withdrawing risperidone, Jean was described in her records: *agitated, extremely restless, yelling, following writer around during room check, very paranoid, gesture to hit staff, pointing finger at writer, unable to reason or communicate with her, at nursing station resident picked up folders and books—threw them on floor, unmanageable... banging on all other residents rooms, finally calmed down @ 630hrs.* She was reported as up and pacing the halls at night. There was no recognition in these records that Jean's so-called behaviour was symptomatic of risperidone toxicity and a discontinuation syndrome associated with this drug. At the time I was not informed of these reports in her records, but told by the facility's acting director that the facility had already made the decision to refer her to a geriatric psychiatry unit at a nearby hospital, because her "aggression must be controlled." I saw nothing of this aggression when I was with her. I received a copy of the facility's letter to this psychiatry unit, which stated, "... there have been a number of incidents in recent months when (Jean's) actions have injured and/or put other residents at unacceptable risk. (Her doctor) has unsuccessfully tried pharmaceutical management. (Jean) was reassessed by our long-term care liaison who has stated that (Jean) would be best managed at a Special Care Unit, these behaviours will not be tolerated at Special Care either. (Note: this reassessment was made by the long term care liaison in October, 1993, based on one nurse's incident reports. RNABC indicated that this nurse was verbally disciplined as a result of my formal complaints regarding the subjectivity, bias, and incompleteness of her records that became the basis for this reassessment at that time.) In addition to the aggression, she has also had several incidents of wandering from the facility.... We have recommended that (Jean) be admitted for geriatric assessment, which will hopefully result in a better management plan. In addition we are recommending to the long-term care liaison that (Jean) be priority waitlisted to a special care-secured unit. It may be the outcome of the assessment that she will no longer wander or be aggressive. However, this is unclear at this time. What is clear and has been clear for several months is that (the facility) cannot safely manage this resident.... We are asking that you treat this referral in an urgent manner. If you are unable to respond to this referral in the immediate future please advise (her doctor) at once as we have indicated an alternate referral, somewhere else, perhaps Riverview, is necessary."

This letter was signed by a nurse who was acting as the director of care at this time, and a social worker. The "unsuccessful medical treatment" referred to in this letter was the neuroleptic risperidone, given to Jean for thirteen days and then suddenly withdrawn because of its serious effects on her. The long-term care liaison, not otherwise connected with this facility, told me at this time, "This is not for your mother's benefit, but so the system can manage her," adding, "There is nothing I can do." I felt Jean's welfare was under more serious threat than ever before. In three weeks time I was to be away for a two-month period, exploring family history, the untold stories of foremothers barely recorded in the archives. If I went, I would be leaving Jean alone for June and July. When I told Jean about going back to Scotland, she had clapped her hands together in delight, and I realized she was happy for me, for what I was doing, writing the stories of the women, her mother, her grandmother. She appeared to me to understand what I was attempting to do, was pleased and interested. For a painful moment I wanted to take her with me. I was assailed by doubts, worry about Jean, in the overwhelm of that time, as Jean continued to exhibit the toxic effects of her drugging. My heart and mind remained unsettled about leaving Jean at that moment in time. There was in me a sense of something important back there for me to find, but whether it was the right time to go, I will likely never be entirely sure.

Before I was to leave, *incident reports* continued: *restlessness, insomnia, confusion, talking to self and irritable, verbally abusive at times, up all night ... wandering in the hallways ... trying to get into other residents' rooms ...* Could she not have been trying to find her own? "Where is home?" she would ask me, later, when there was only morphine to ease her pain. Right then, what was being witnessed appeared to me to be the classic symptoms of delirium, toxicity from the drugs she was given. She was reported: *verbally disruptive to one other resident in w/c* (wheel chair). *Staff member states she "took hold of the wheel chair, when asked to leave resident she* (Jean) *struck me on my arm 3 times mod. hard," no bruise noted @ present.* I was rarely or never informed of these incidents as they were described in her records. Care aides seemed to avoid saying anything. Nursing staff, when I asked, when they were available, would tell me they "would have to check her records," or sometimes referred to her as "agitated," or not. Occasionally an individual nurse would provide some concern and insight regarding Jean.

Shortly before I was to leave the province, two members of the geriatric psychiatry unit arrived at the facility to assess Jean. Based on an hour alone with her and whatever information facility staff had provided, the psychiatrist, accompanied by a psychiatric social worker, informed me that Jean was "calm, friendly and completely disoriented, is wearing four skirts, one on top of the other." Yes, I replied, she often does. Her short-term memory, you know. The psychiatrist's look of pleasant amusement became bemused. He looked down and became esoteric, naming the drugs he was considering "using on Jean." I objected, mentioning the already deleterious effects on Jean of such drugs. He admitted these drugs were "poisons in the body," but stated it "was a matter of balancing the poisoning with the amount of drug required to manage Jean." His letter, which I found later in Jean's records, stated that Jean had been referred to him for: ... *assessment of increased agitation and unpredictable aggression, although there has been a long-standing history of episodes of verbal and physical aggression, there appears to have been a recent exacerbation over the past several weeks. According to the staff and the patient's family ... is having difficulty with decreased sleep, poor appetite, and increasing episodes of aggression and agitation. These episodes are unpredictable in nature and ... apparently the patient has not complained of being in any pain and between these episodes of agitation does not appear to be in any distress ... she talked about her mother being alive and denied that she had any children. She was completely disoriented to place and time and seemingly unaware that she was wearing four skirts. The patient denied any thoughts of aggression or self-harm, and denied any distress or pain. In addition to her profound disorientation ... demonstrated numerous other cognitive difficulties including constructional apraxia* (inability to draw or build simple constructions) *and language difficulties ... environmental management of her difficult behaviour has not been successful therefore I would suggest the addition of trazodone starting at 100mg. daily ... also suggest she be put on a waitlist for admission to ... Geriatric Psychiatry Unit.... Pharmacological trials could be initiated more easily on an inpatient basis as well....Thank you for this most interesting referral....* Jean was now referred to, not as a resident, but as a patient. The "family," that is, myself, did not report increased episodes of aggression or refer to Jean as aggressive, never saw her in this state when with her. What I saw at this point, and communicated to this psychiatrist and psychiatric social worker with him, was a marked deterioration in Jean's overall health and physical well-being. I saw a reduction in her physical strength and abilities that was rapid and coincided with her being given anti-psychotic and anti-anxiety drugs. I could see the noticeable increase of confusion, disorientation, and difficulty with speech. I also was aware that Jean was experiencing some kind of pain in her neck, was listing to the side, both left and right in her gait, sometimes backwards, and often to the front, shuffling and almost running forward, when we went for walks or I observed her walking in the halls.

I did not see or experience any anger from her, or aggressive acts, or hostility while with her. I saw agitation when I first began assisting, then again, to begin with, when helping Jean on my own with her bathing. This agitation I recognized as a possible fear of damage to her eyes (her experience of being almost blind due to glaucoma and cataracts before lens implant surgery), and because of her sudden cries from time to time when I was washing or combing her hair, that she was experiencing pain in her neck and body. I had communicated this to staff. I took steps to work around these and communicated the possibility of pain as well as these other issues on several occasions to staff. There appears to have been nothing communicated between staff in their daily records, although I, on at least two occasions, wrote letters in detail on all of these issues as well as others, which, although placed in her file, did not seem to have been read.

It was indicated to me by the psychiatrist during his interview with me, that other anti-psychotic and anti-anxiety drugs would be used if necessary to "manage her aggression." I requested there would also be an assessment of what changes could be made in her care and environment that would be beneficial *for her* and reduce stress for both Jean and staff. And wrote long and detailed suggestions in a letter of understanding, stating I wished Jean to remain where she was at least until I returned at the end of July. Told there was "no option left but to control Jean's behaviour with drugs," what I had seen thus far were adverse effects *from* these drugs and their toxic effects on Jean used to reinforce an ongoing attitude towards her, that she was, as the facility described her in their letter to the psychiatry unit, "unmanageable and the source of unprovoked and unpredictable aggression." That she was the source of the problem. This was their rationale for removing her, involuntarily, to a secure geriatric psychiatry unit where she would, again involuntarily, be given several anti-psychotic drugs. Eventually this rationale would be called into question by the unit's psychiatric nursing staff (not the psychiatrists).

I had no access to Jean's records at that time, did not know what was being written, or omitted, regarding Jean, and had only the word of facility staff for what they said was happening when I was not with her. I was aware the facility now saw me as uncooperative and were no longer "consulting" with me. What discussions we had appeared to have little bearing on what they intended to do. In my letter requesting she remain at the facility while I was away, I tried to avoid an impression of being uncooperative, concerned as to how this might affect Jean. When I found my letter in Jean's records after her death I was appalled at how I "took on" some of the language that was being used to describe Jean. It seemed like such a forlorn attempt on my part to keep her out of the geriatric psychiatry unit, at least until I returned. What I did not understand at that time was that no one at the care facility or the geriatric psychiatry unit needed my permission to do anything. What was needed was my being on record as agreeing to this committal, and naively, I did just that, hoping to appear cooperative, and keep Jean's options open, by requesting, as I had been asked to do, that her name remain on the wait-list for in-patient assessment but, I added, if she appeared to be adjusting to the medications prescribed, when the dosages were adjusted to what she could take without harmful side effects, that she remain at the facility and be observed in her familiar surroundings by staff to whom I had already given a letter outlining approaches needed regarding her personal care, etc., particularly as her only relative and contact, myself, would suddenly not be there anymore for two months. In the event of her being an in-patient, I had asked, how much control would family have over what testing she would be given? I received no answer. My letter put me on record as *requesting my mother's involuntary admission,* and my words were quoted back to me in future investigations concerning my formal complaints about what was done to her in this psychiatric unit.

At this moment, late spring 1999, as I was writing this, my son called me from Ontario, on his little daughter's first birthday. She had been crawling on hands and knees, appeared around a corner, looked up at him, and for a moment he saw an expression there on her face that reminded him of his grandmother Jean, his daughter's great grandmother. He wanted to let me know. And so Jean's presence returned to me in many ways and at different times—sometimes a crow came to the tree outside my window and hung out there, it seemed, until I was back on track telling this story, which was taking me places I sometimes didn't wish to go, but must.

Endless Roof of Sky

May 31, 1994, on the orders of the referring psychiatrist from the geriatric psychiatry unit, Jean was given two drugs, trazodone and Xanax (alprazolam), both at higher dosages than the cautionary dosages indicated in the literature for those over sixty years of age. For those over sixty years trazodone comes with the warning: *watch for restlessness, agitation, excitement, forgetfulness, confusion, disorientation and an unsteady gait ... adverse effects include anger, hostility, impaired memory, delusions, hallucinations, irregular heart rhythm, nightmares and lowered blood pressure, fainting. Over dosage is marked by drowsiness, weakness, confusion, tremors, low blood pressure, rapid heart rate, stupor. Dosage for those over 60 years should not exceed half of that recommended for adults: 50 mg., 3x/day, ie., a total of 75mg/day....* Jean's dose of trazodone was begun at 100 mg/day. Trazodone is one of a group of anti-depressants implicated in a study of paradoxical effects that demonstrate increased symptoms of depression, and which are known to cause life-threatening cardiovascular problems much more frequently in older persons.

Xanax (alprazolam), given to Jean at the same time, is a tranquillizer of the benzodiazepine type, a short-acting, high-potency drug associated with more frequent and intensive adverse drug reactions ranging from short-term memory impairment and confusion to delirium, behavioural reactions, some of the worst occurring during withdrawal of the drug, or between doses, or in its aftermath. Described as the mechanism for producing behavioural abnormalities, reference handbooks to alert physicians to adverse drug reactions, each indicate that mania and uncontrollable rage are special problems with Xanax. Short-acting benzodiazepines such as Xanax were the drug of choice for elderly patients until it was found that they induced rebound insomnia (a worsening) on discontinuation of the drug (a hypnotic), as well as rebound anxiety, anterograde amnesia and even paradoxical rage. As well, the literature indicates elderly patients have been found to be prone to the central nervous system depressant activity of benzodiazepines, even at low doses, and cautions adverse reactions of over-sedation, hypotension and neurological impairment could result, and initial dosages should be low, 0.25 to 0.375 mg per day. Jean, ninety years old, was given 0.5 mg per day from the outset. Withdrawal symptoms observed after abrupt discontinuation of this drug included irritability, nervousness, insomnia, agitation, and mental impairment, among others. These two drugs, given to Jean at this point, were later withdrawn suddenly and replaced with others. Xanax has been found to interact with digoxin, increasing the effects of digoxin and producing symptoms of digoxin toxicity, among these: dizziness, lack of coordination, drowsiness, release of hostility and other paradoxical effects, including irritability, excitability and hallucinations ... headache, fatigue, blurred vision, nausea, confusion, depression, increase or decrease in blood sugar levels ... disorientation, difficulty reading and mental changes that can be mistaken for senile dementia or psychosis.

After Jean was given the above two drugs on May 31, 1994, the following notes appeared in her records:

June 2, 1994: *found in her bathroom attempting to remove her stockings but unable to due to drowsiness. Gait unsteady. Speech slow and slightly slurred. Cooperative. Assisted to bed by 2 persons ....*

June 4, 1994: *resident pleasant and cooperative this p.m. Daughter in to visit and showered her....*

June 7, 1994: *resident's gait unsteady @ times. Leaning to L. side. Daughter also notices slurred speech.*

June 8, 1994: *6:00 a.m. awake but quiet in her room most of the night shift, became agitated restless and paranoid at 6:00 a.m. Came to N. (nursing) Station pointing finger at resident and staff for no reason.*

This last entry is signed by the same RN, referred to earlier regarding her subjective reports about Jean.

June 8, 1994, I was leaving for two months. Staff had not given me any of these details, as they appeared in Jean's records for that time. I had mentioned to them I thought her speech was slurred. The urgency I felt to make this journey to retrieve family history faltered, as I questioned whether I was abandoning my mother at that moment, whether it was me that was going missing to search for a story to tell myself, or was my perception of her need of me something child-learned, part of a small child's fear of abandonment. Would there be a story to tell Jean in which the pieces would flow together freely, unfettered, as watercolours flow, shape shifting into new shades of understanding, the spaciousness of what feels true? I had, again, written detailed descriptions of how to approach and assist Jean, in the hope, in spite of all the evidence to the contrary, that all those involved in her care would be understanding of her needs. Would these be read? I had been bringing in cut flowers to augment the flowers in her garden outside her window, and made arrangements with a local store to deliver flowers each week I would be away. When I explained the situation, the woman serving me told me her father had just died. While I was away she personally looked after the weekly delivery, enclosing a card for me each time.

At the door to Jean's room, as I left, telling her I would send her lots of postcards, she did something I had no memory of her ever doing. She held me in her arms in a long hug, told me to take care of myself, and kissed my cheek. Jean standing, erect, in her doorway; I did not know I would never see her like this again.

June 9, 1994, the day after I left, a nurse wrote in Jean's records: *Resident wandered out of facility approx. ½ blk east of here. C.A.*(care aide) *attempted to bring her back but unsuccessful. R.N. went to assist & brought resident back with much persuasion, aggression.* Five days later her doctor wrote in Jean's records: *decrease trazodone slightly for ?drugged effect.*

After my departure I called the facility regularly. At one point I was told Jean's blood pressure had been dropping, at another time that she was coughing up greenish mucous. I was not told that the trazodone has been decreased from 100 mg/day to 75 mg daily, or why. By

June 23, I was in Scotland, searching the national archives housed in stone, searching for my grandmother Jane and the women who came before her, in the names of their fathers and husbands, and within the week had traced my maternal grandmother Jane to the village of Currie, Scotland. I was there, staring at a small one-room stone cottage where Jane lived as a baby and small girl, a farm labourer's cottage, one of many clustered around the stone kirk, built by the Knights Templar several hundreds of years ago, Templar bones buried within kirk walls. Jane's mother Marion and father Robert were likely both itinerant farm labourers, people of the land, Marion perhaps from Flemish weavers migrating west out of continental Europe, escaping the Inquisition. The census described Jane's father at that time as Land Steward. This same day in Vancouver, a social worker left the following message in Jean's records: *Issue: Resident agitation and restlessness. Jean on first floor refusing to leave reception area stating she has to leave the bldg. Observed resident to be very upset, appearing to be threatened, babbling about all she needs to do & not do, nonsensical conversation. walked ...x 20 minutes, no physical contact, reassured her requests "to pick things up" would be cared for. Resident expressing fear and angry at people "talking too much, too much noise." Jean requires as calming an environment as possible. Whenever possible if she can have non-intrusive one to one time during these episodes it may decrease agitation, tendency to strike out. Plan discussed with R.N. my query if there is a need for PRN med. for this resident.* PRN medication mentioned here referred to orders for extra dosages of a prescribed medication, as needed, in the judgement of nursing staff.

I discovered my grandmother Jane's birthplace in Edinburgh, a scant two blocks from the hostel where I was staying on Princes Street, near Haymarket Station, where gulls flew up with an explosive snapping of wings, as though into a troubled sky. The address on Jane's birth record was a street name that no longer existed. It took a few hours of record searching by a helpful librarian to find its current name, locate it, along a curve of road I had passed many times. I took pictures for Jean, but lost the film, which was probably just as well. It was soot-darkened building of abandoned flats, pasted over with poster ads for a Rolling Stones concert. I could find no record in the Edinburgh archives of Jane's marriage to my grandfather, and travelled to the southwest coast of Scotland to where his birth record said he'd been born, but found little specific information there, instead, a car dealership where his birth place may have been, a history of high and low church, industrialization, and witnessed a frightening episode of a drunken physical assault in a mall, pop bottles and their contents sliding across gleaming floor tiles and U2 playing on the intercom. In Vancouver, Jean's records continued: *resident wandered off premises....Brought back ... with some persuasion.*

It was now July and what were referred to as Jean's *behaviours are to be observed* PRN *dosages of current medications as necessary since decrease in trazodone.* I had returned from Britain, was in Toronto by then, staying with my son, while checking the Ontario archives. It was here where I found Jane's name on a passenger list for the liner *Carthaginian*, which had embarked from Liverpool for Montreal, Canada, in 1885, with her a three-year-old son, named William, after his father, my grandfather. Jane was listed as unmarried. My grandfather had been in Canada since 1882, homesteading land in southwest Manitoba. Jane arrived the fall Louis Riel was hanged in Regina. She and William were married in January, 1886. While here, I received a long-distance call from Jean's doctor and was told that Jean had broncho-pneumonia and was being given antibiotics. Facility records described Jean at that time as: *ill, feverish, lethargic, not eating, restless and very confused, up at 0300 hrs wearing only underwear, enters another resident's room, grabs her feet and then leaves ... agitated and aggressive when* CA(care aide) + *nurse put her gown on and refused to wear it, taking her blanket ... out of her room, stating "it doesn't belong to me," left in her room, settled to bed ... confused, restless, wandering into other residents' rooms ... she is found sleeping in another resident's room and fairly cooperative when asked to leave* ... and that, on July 18, 1994, the care facility had requested admission of Jean to the geriatric psychiatry unit. The next day staff noted an incident they described: *No obvious injuries noted... aggression unprovoked and unpredictable, punched and kicked another female resident several times.* I was by then preparing to leave Ontario for Manitoba and Jean's birthplace, and had been staying, at that point, with my daughter and son-in-law who were living west of Toronto. While there, I had borrowed their car to travel to my father's birthplace in a small town along the St. Lawrence River. There I discovered he was the eldest of a family of five. His father had been adopted, either while in London, England, or after coming to Canada, at what age and under what circumstances was unknown. My father had been given his father's birth family's name as a middle name. I found the graves of his younger brother, killed in the first world war, at age eighteen, and his sister, who died at nineteen of a kidney disease. Learned, much later, that he had cared for his younger brother, the youngest, when the family broke apart, working as a mill worker, office help, and farm labourer, until he was able to complete his high school at nineteen, in Winnipeg, and went on to college there and then to war. My father's mother had descended from early Irish and Scots who settled along the St Lawrence River; her own mother had died when she was still a child, and then her father when she was twelve. I found a copy of her father's will in the Ontario archives, in which he left provision for her education, the property to his sons, and furniture and household effects to his daughter, my grandmother, Isabella. Both my father and mother had carried many sorrows.

The night before I was to leave for Manitoba, I received another long-distance call and was told Jean would be admitted involuntarily to the psychiatry unit the following day. I would be home in ten days, but in spite of my calls to the unit's psychiatric social worker, and the acting director at the care facility, to delay this until I returned, this involuntary admission took place July 26, 1994, by ambulance. On admission to this psychiatry unit, Jean's records described her as *pleasant and relaxed*. I found, later, when I had returned to Vancouver, the contents of her dresser drawers spilled and scattered over the floor of her room at the care facility, as though some kind of struggle had taken place. I had gone there to take her clothing to her at the psychiatry unit, as I had been told by nursing staff at the unit that no clothing had been brought with her, nor any sent over later.

During the first ten days of Jean's involuntary committal I was searching for her past in Manitoba. I had arranged previously to stay at a farmhouse bed and breakfast, which was the only accommodation available within miles of this very small town where Jean grew up. When I first arrived, the bed and breakfast had an abandoned feel to it, the owner in the next town at a baseball game, her note of welcome told me, along with which room I could use, and that she would be by sometime the next day. She lived somewhere else. I stood surrounded by fields of alfalfa running to endless roof of sky, to the east beyond them, the town a distant mirage glowing in salmon light from an already setting sun, blood red where it sank behind a meandering stream and its poplar scrub, behind the house. Mosquitoes drove me inside. I wandered around the large house, uneasy, feeling an odd sense of abandonment, an angry panic, and trying to make up my mind whether to get back in my rented car and drive away from there, back to Winnipeg, cut short my trip and go home. The phone rang, a psychiatrist from the unit, wanting information about Jean. I had left this number with the hospital. She wanted family history. I was suddenly afraid of words, how mine might wound Jean, no matter what I said. What had brought me to here, searching this sense of something waiting for me, us; could I call this a coming home, there through a sleepless night tracing a full moon's transient light across an unfamiliar room, wail of a prairie freight train crossing distance out of time?

Shadow of the Sun

July 26,1994: *clean, neat, appropriately groomed, continent, with understandable speech, an appropriate affect/mood, with notable anxiety/tearfulness* .... was how Jean's admittance to the geriatric psychiatry unit was described in her records. Jean's perception of admission was described as: *"no not right now," "They asked me to come."* Her breathing was recorded as: *normal, regular,* her level of consciousness: *alert,* her heart sounds: *normal,* rhythm: *irregular.* Jean's *allergy/adverse drug reaction update* had only: ASA? There were no cautions regarding drugs, no mention at all of Jean having been taken off BuSpar and risperidone due to the adverse effects of these drugs on her, her sensitivity to them. She is also described as: *oriented to person but not to place or time, with no insight into illness or hospitalization ... very confused and easily agitated. May need calm/reassuring/quiet approach for easiest communication.* She had become a *patient.*

Jean's admitting history was recorded by a resident in psychiatry working under the supervision of a more senior psychiatrist, whom I never would meet. Based on information provided by Jean's care facility, her history stated: *aggressive behaviour going back to 1990, she apparently had been aggressive enough in that she was alleged to have injured several careworkers at her place of residence.* A clinical trainee wrote: *in 1990 this aggressive behaviour was observed for the first time. She was treated with Loxapine for a short period of time, but she developed some extra pyramidal symptoms and Loxapine was discontinued.* But, of course, Jean was living in her own home in 1990, did not injure homemakers, did not enter the care facility until February of 1992, where loxapine was given as single dose on one or two separate occasions prior to my being aware of it. Her doctor subsequently ordered that no anti-psychotics be given to her.

Jean's first day in the psychiatry unit was described in nursing notes: *Considerably confused and disoriented. Agitation is evident but pt. responds to calm reassurance ... needing frequent re-orientation ... voicing vague suspiciousness/ paranoia. Not answering questions and stating we're "going to tell all the other people." Appears bright, good affect, confused, disoriented, thought she was at home, talkative, speech irrelevant to question, doesn't know why she is admitted to hospital, not accepting nurse's explanation ... refuses having her vital signs taken and also any medication, stated nurse gave her pills to kill her.* At this point Jean had been given trazodone, reduced from 100mg/day to 75 mg/day and Xanax (alprazolam) 0.25 mg/day for 26 days, begun May 31 at the care facility, along with digoxin 0.125 mg/day. In addition she was given 0.5mg Ativan *for agitation* the evening of the day she was admitted to this psychiatric unit. Ativan, or lorazepam is a benzodiazepine with similar effects as the alprazolam (Xanax) she is already on. The assault all the previously administered drugs had already made on Jean, on her cognition, short-term memory impairment, confusion, and delirium would be increased. Behavioural abnormalities directly attributable to these drugs, including withdrawal and rebound syndromes, where anxiety and insomnia and other serious emotional effects occur and intensify, would all appear, and be assumed to be coming from what was perceived as Jean's "dementia," her "unpredictable and unprovoked aggression" and therefore dosage increases and additional drugs would be considered necessary to control "her behaviour." Not surprisingly, the following morning, July 27, after Ativan was given the night previous, nursing notes indicated Jean was *difficult to rouse ++sedated this a.m. required total assist with all adl's and ambulation, breakfast taken poorly d/t drowsiness...short hypotensive period.* This noted hypotensive period, the literature states, is an indication of serious overdose. Jean was also incontinent for the first time in her life, when voiding urine. She would remain so. By mid-afternoon nurses describe Jean: *Confused and disoriented, speech logical in form often nonsensical in content except for short 1-2-word sentences. She refuses an* ECG *struck out at nurse during attempts and later stated that she could see "chickens" on staff's shoulder's, knows they shouldn't be there but sees them anyways* (anyway).

I had not slept that first night in Manitoba. No other farms visible from a window of this farmhouse, half a mile from the highway, through circling fields of alfalfa. To the east was a line of distant trees and the grain elevator of the town where I hoped to find fragments of Jean's history. A night spent in vigilant listening, tracing patterns of light on unfamiliar shapes, nerves caught up in haunting wails of trains moving through too large a space left me less than gracious when the owner arrived, asked if I'd slept well. Not at all, I'd replied. When she offered to stay over the next night, that she could see how a city person could find the isolation a little strange, I felt embarrassed, like a child, which right then I pretty much was. Silently she pointed to the dining room window, which overlooked a large garden, a doe with her fawn there, poised in morning light, only their white tails flicking. I moved to look, and startled, they disappeared into the willows along the stream. I felt awkward, jumpy. The garden the deer had just left I had not seen until then, a large one full of vegetables, flowers. I thought then of Jane's, and felt an anchoring. My host made me breakfast, said she had a few hours, and offered to help me find what I needed. What are you looking for? she had asked. I realized that was what I was here to find out. I followed her car to town and the municipal office, was again given variations on what had been sent me, my grandfather, his prize-winning wheat, all the farming and agricultural associations he belonged to, his ten sons, their service in the First Great War, deaths, burials in the local cemetery, a brief reference to Jean, the daughter, and, again, no reference at all to her mother Jane, other than a passing nod as *wife* of my grandfather. My guide asked at the museum if we might find the old family farm. We were given a handful of copies of old survey maps, and I followed the dust of my B&B owner's car in my own Sunbird rental, through a maze of concession roads I could never have navigated on my own, past fields of sunflowers, their heads all turned to face the sun. If I got lost here, could I navigate by the sun, by the sunflowers, to find my way to the remains of an abandoned farm

Jean's family homestead.

that township maps had indicated was the homestead where Jean grew up? Could I find my way back again?

The original house was still there, and the trees Jean's father planted to break the wind, twisted and turned on themselves. The house, returning to earth, seemed much too small to have housed them all. One window stared at me, shreds of curtains hanging from an eye milky with dust and mould and reflecting dark images back at me, of those trees, stunted, bent over by wind and winter snows. I searched about among weeds, wild grasses I had no names for, searched for signs of Jane's garden. I remembered Jean's words about the heat that was all around out there, beyond those trees, felt the sun's heat pressing on my head. At the car rental in Winnipeg, I had been told "you don't want to be out there driving the prairie without airconditioning." The doe and her fawn, early morning in the garden, the deer were good swimmers, but didn't do well in heat; where, on this prairie, would they go to escape it; where had they come from? Aside from heat, too long winters, too deep snow, what other threats were theirs to survive? My guide gave me a sense she knew much, was saying little, letting me find out for myself, reminded me to take photos. I had forgotten the camera hanging from my shoulder. Then she led me to the one living relative who had remained in the area. This cousin, a decade older than I, now lived in a shack on a brow of land, with two miniature Clydesdale horses, curious beings who peered at me from around either side of him. A batchelor, nearly blind, who had no phone, who wouldn't move into town because he would have to give up his horses. He had good memories of visits with Jean in Winnipeg. I didn't remember these visits. I remembered him from my stay on my uncle's farm when I was ten. It was probably meant to be a summer in the country for me, but after a few weeks I'd come home, ill and unhappy, but couldn't tell my mother I'd been teased and harassed, not by this cousin, who was quiet and older than the others, but by younger brothers, one, a wild sixteen-year-old who tried to scare me by choking me. They put me bareback on a pony and sent it galloping out onto a hard-packed dirt pasture, where I promptly slid off into a collision of head and shoulder with earth. My aunt said nothing as I hobbled around, my back so sore I could barely straighten up. When I became sick, they sent me home. I doubt Jean was ever told what happened.

I was led back through another dusty labyrinth of concession roads to the town's municipal hall and, on my own now, wandered about

Jean's mother Jane, an early photo.

in the small attached museum. There was a map showing an Indian reserve that had been in the area but no longer existed. Jean once told me her mother Jane had given tea to Indians who came to the door, and Jean, afraid or shy, had hidden behind her mother's skirts. I went into the office to ask them why the farm had been abandoned—all those prizes for wheat, all those sons? Was there not more information available? A student working there for the summer went to look in their local family files. There seemed to be some hesitation, a silent exchange of looks, before a file card was slipped down the counter toward me, as though it didn't belong. I picked it up, read there what I already knew, until a note written in faint pencil down at the bottom of the card told another, a different story, from the spaces between the rows in Jane's garden. In February, 1901, a report appeared in a small Manitoba town newspaper. Jean's father had been brought before Magistrate's Court, charged with assault of her mother, fined and bound over to keep the peace for one year. There was no indication of who brought the charges. Jean's mother had nine sons then, a tenth would be born a year later and her youngest and last child, her only daughter, Jean, would be born New Year's Day, 1904. I felt it then, why I was impelled to take this journey, not away from Jean but toward her, to her, still leading the way for me to follow.

I found myself driving towards a prairie horizon of thunderheads climbing a sky dissolving into haze, north to a hospital to see a woman I was told grew up with Jean and had remained all her life in this town, running a family business, in hospital because she had broken her hip. She was the one who had set up the museum files on local families, had pencilled in the note.

"Sit down, I'm going to tell you the truth," she said, fixing her very blue eyes on me. I felt as though I was looking into the face of an eagle. She was still angry with Jean for leaving Jane and this town seventy years ago and never returning. "Oh, perhaps once," she added, pausing, "before her mother died, but not for her funeral. Can you understand that? After all she did for them?" Apparently some of Jane's sons did not return, either. Her anger smacked up against me, reverberated. A "prominent drunk" was how she described my grandfather who died, she said, when Jean was seventeen. Jean and Jane had been taken away from the farm by her oldest brothers, to live in town with them, some years before, to protect them from him. I remembered, then, Jean telling me last winter, when she began to speak of her father, that he

Jean, perhaps twelve.

had "stayed out on the farm on his own, never lived in town with them, the boys quietly left for jobs somewhere else." Jean thought that she was "maybe ten, or eleven," when she and her mother went to live in town. As the story of Jean continued, in that hospital room, in the heat of a small Manitoba town under a bowl of sky that seemed to hold everything—the farm, eventually auctioned off, her mother Jane left in poverty—I saw Jean in my mind, returning from Winnipeg, from dreams of an education there, gone, left with normal school and country school teaching, in towns steeped in a dreary Calvinism that pinched life between its fingers. I was overwhelmed with what Jean had carried all those years, how much her silence must have been her survival, how necessary to protect herself from a childhood and adolescence filled with fear, shame, and harm. Leaving it all behind, running for her life, suppressing fear and memory, in order to be able to go on. Jean was of an age and a generation of those who were taught not to speak of these things, women in particular learned to be silent. But the fear and anxiety Jean must have been forced to learn as a child, in a situation she couldn't control, but to which she had to adapt, would be stored deep in body cells, memory; that the body remembers now recognized as the basis for post trauma flashbacks in later life, such as during the retrieval of long-term memories. I looked at this eagle of a woman and said I could understand why my mother had to leave like that, and explained a little of what Jean was going through. The eagle's eyes, her voice, softened and she said, "You bring another point of view."

Grieving Bodies

Jean had been in the psychiatric unit for two days when trazodone, reduced, previous to her admission to this unit, because of its adverse effect on Jean, was increased to the original dosage of 100 mg/day for "aggression." At this point nursing notes described Jean as *continues paranoid and suspicious, doesn't want to take her meds, says "I'm fine, I don't need it, you just want to kill me," ... very confused making suspisious* (as spelled) *remarks: "people will talk about me" ... continuing incontinent, stating she is tired but declining to rest, refusing having her vital signs tested, saying "I can't handle it," carrying on conversation with nurses on very superficial level. Nine p.m. found fallen down in the hallway because of pain in both knees, states "it's only a little sore." Unsteady gait and assisted to bed....* twenty-four hours later, nursing staff noted over the day: *continuing confused and unsteady on feet, declining to rest in spite of stating frequently "I'm tired," and "I don't know where to go," incontinent and trying to take off her clothing in the hallway, resisting care .... able to talk about missing daughter ... continues to miss daughter ... walking in hallway talking out loud, speech confused, resistant to bed ... ten p.m., resistant during care, raising voice and pushing away, aggression.* After a full night's sleep Jean was described *assisting with a.m. care, able to help when given direction, very sensitive and stating often, "it hurts" during care.* At this point loxapine "for aggression" was added to the drugs being given Jean and she received two doses over that day, July30.

Neuroleptics , such as loxapine, and others that Jean had been given to this point, were known to cause brain dysfunctions of motor control, such as painful muscle spasms in head and neck and also in other areas. The spasms can affect any voluntary muscles, including those of speech, swallowing, breathing, and gait, cause motor restlessness impelling the person to keep moving their body. This can show itself externally or remain inside the individual as a painful inner tension and anxiety. Behavioural symptoms of this may then be misdiagnosed as due to the person's psychosis or dementia, chronic anxiety, or agitated depression. It is reported that these extra pyramidal syndromes, as they are referred to, occur in "up to 90% of those given these drugs, and that these drugs are then continued or increased under the mistaken assumption that toxic drug reaction is indicative of psychiatric disorder, and that these neuro-toxic effects become even more frequent and disabling in the elderly." Individual responses to these neuroleptic-induced disorders are described as extreme fatigue to the point of exhaustion and psychological suffering, as well as withdrawal syndromes. Such drugs, as were given to Jean, are described as sharing "... the capacity to produce generalized dysfunction with some degree of impairment across the spectrum of emotional and intellectual function. Because the brain is so highly integrated, it is not possible to disable circumscribed mental functions without impairing a variety of them."

By the middle of the morning on July 30, nursing notes described Jean *talking to herself and repeatedly stating "I don't know where to go,"* or *"I want to go home" easy to settle but unable to retain any information given.* By early afternoon: *unsteady, remaining so and appears weak in the knees ... found urinating on the floor in front of the nursing station and assisted to bed, continues urinating on the floor and continually complaining of leg pain ... talking to self ... an occasional relevant statement ... speech remains confused with repetition of phrases....* And so ended her fourth day in this psychiatric unit. I would observe, on my return in six more days, that new admissions to this unit appeared to respond to the chemicals they were

Remembered home.

given with incontinency, disorientation, taking off clothing, pacing the halls, wandering in a lost sort of way, becoming distraught, angry.

In Manitoba, on that day, I had driven a couple of hundred kilometres north of where Jean was born, with a sense of urgency to get back to her. My guide, who owned the bed and breakfast where I had stayed, had gone down into the cellar the night before, to bake loaves of bread in a stove there, where it was cooler, for me to take that morning. Her help had been essential to locating Jean's history, and Jane's, in that town, where, I had begun to feel, there may have been disapproval of my grandmother Jane, not my grandfather, perhaps an opinion of the time that she had brought this on herself by coming here, with an *illegitimate* son, to find my grandfather, hunting him down. When he died, she was referred to as his relict.

I had gone north, looking for that small hamlet where I spent the first five years of my life, found it had all but disappeared back into poplar trees and scrub brush. I had driven past several times without seeing it, until finally I flagged down a truck I met on the road to ask directions. You passed it, the driver told me. But there was just a sign, I protested. That's it, he said, smiled, and motioned me to follow. At what had by then become a familiar corner, he pointed toward a small wooden sign nailed to a tree, and disappeared behind veils of dust. A woman walking her dog appeared along the road, a pathologist from Winnipeg, who had come there to look after a relative who had become ill. What's left is down there, she told me, pointing toward what I saw for the first time, a road curving off between the poplar trees, past a modern bungalow on the corner that, as I learned, used to be where the post office was. Around the curve, as though waiting for me, the house appeared, as it had been in my memory, the only structure left of what was once there, from what I could see, except for a community centre bearing the architecture of its ancestry as a small wooden church I remembered. Our former house was dwarfed by what had been two little spruce trees in our front yard. The little window, from where I had looked out at the world, looked down on me. Some kind of thick, green crop surrounded the house. I didn't want to go any closer, engulfed suddenly in a miasma of lost memories, lost childhoods, sadness, longing for what went missing. I remembered the snake, squatting or standing over it in that backyard, mesmerized by the beauty of the glowing patterns of its skin, a large snake. I can't remember what happened after that, except for the aftermath, when fascination and fear became tangled, and Jean was telling me my father said not to be afraid. Which was honest, as she feared snakes. Gone was the blacksmith's shop, where my father retrieved me from underneath a horse being shod, and I remembered my surprise, as it hadn't occurred to me the horse would do me harm. I was expecting something to be waiting here for me, something not yet understood, did not know why I retreated from going nearer the house through that surrounding of unfamiliar green thick-stalked vegetation, stood staring at windows clouded with disuse. A man mowing grass around the new bungalow on the corner where the post office used to be, had stopped, was watching me. Our gazes connected for a moment. I drove away, with a backward look at the house, grieving what I didn't understand, or even know, that remained beyond conscious recall, a body grieving, knowing what it alone knows. A quick succession of images overtook me. Jean putting out a pan of oatmeal at the bottom of the garden for the wild ducks who came, Jean bandaging the injured paw of a wandering farm dog, planting her vegetable garden along the back fence, a frozen pump at the kitchen sink, frost on kitchen linoleum, bells jingling on the huge horses pulling barrels of water on flat sleighs over a landscape gone white and featureless, where army snow "bombadiers" buzzed and whined in a child's empty forever. I passed an empty field where my father's school had been, the grain elevator gone; no trains came through here anymore. A few bungalows of more recent vintage were scattered here and there among the trees, and up on a hill, cut poplar stacked, firewood drying for the winter ahead. Drier than those logs too green to burn, when Jean needed to melt snow on the woodstove for Saturday afternoon laundry in metal tubs on the kitchen floor, Jean heaving one of them into the wash, and soapy water leaping high into the air, hitting the floor and sliding in foamy waves to where my small feet were waiting on the shore; these were all images with a feel of shards, splintering and binding memory's heart. I drove away from there, first to Dauphin, where I was born in the hospital there, and on to West Hawk Lake, and found the cabins where, after the Second World War ended, and before my father died, we had spent some time, weekends mostly. My mother and I spent a week together on our own there. I forgot to pack my pyjamas and was miserable during the cold nights. When we went for a walk up the hill behind the cabin, I pretended to see a snake. Jean squealed and rushed back down the hill. I wasn't expecting so much reaction, her fright, thinking it would just

be a funny joke, felt guilty. She wasn't angry, a little embarrassed. We
had fun with squirrels and chipmunks that were under the cabin and
forever climbing into empty pails and turning them over, occasionally
getting themselves caught underneath. We would walk down every day
to a dock away from the main beach, lay our towels down on it and lie
in the sun. I would watch my mother, the sky, clouds, birds, dragonflies,
and what I called skater bugs scooting across the surface of water so
full of tadpoles and fish fry I couldn't figure out why I was never able to
reach in and catch any with my hands. The lap of the lake water, so very
blue, gently rocked the dock. I needed to tell Jean I'd been back there.

In Vancouver, on her fifth day in the psychiatry unit, Jean was found
*banging with her shoe on her bed rail, unable to assist with her care,
incontinent, stating numerous times that staff was hurting and/or going
to kill her ... accepting of reassurance but unable to retain information,
oriented to self only, periodic making rational statements but usually
are irrelevant in nature ... response aggression both physical and verbal
when care given, but responded to direction....* Over the remainder of
the day Jean was described variously as *restless, confused, repeatedly
stating that she doesn't know where to go ... maintains good eye
contact, has a good range of affect, her thought process paranoid that
staff were going to harm her ... appearing to hallucinate—carrying
on conversation with someone in her room. .... thought process
delusional, angry ideation....* By evening Jean's speech was described as
*confused and nonsensical ... requires total assist with care and unable
to follow directions, visual hallucinations present, talking angrily to
same, indicating to staff that she can see "a small man" on staff's arm,
aggression, striking out at staff in response to redirection ... intrusive
and threatening.* At this point Jean was given another injection of
loxapine for *agitation and response aggression.* An hour later this
prn dose was deemed effective—Jean was asleep. The following day,
August 1, Jean experienced pain and difficulty walking. Her records
stated: *observed walking stooped over hips and knees flexed ... holding
her groin and saying it hurts ... eyes closed a lot of the time, slow to
open ... asks to be allowed to slip down to the floor ... noticeably
befuddled, her statement incongruent with present situation....* By
August 2, Jean experienced insomnia, agitation, and irritability, and
was described: *non-compliant to meds and being touched.* Later in
the afternoon: *meds given, full range affect....* Half an hour later Jean
was described as *standing at nursing station, intrusive behaviour and*

difficult to redirect. She was then given an injection of loxapine *for agitation,* which was deemed *effective.* Jean was then described as *directable and pleasant.* An hour and a half later she was described: *restless, becoming irritable and non-compliant when approached re incontinence ... affect becomes generally flat ...hallucinating in bed, observed pt.'s arms stretched out to the air asking "but who will look after me?" eyes closed at that time ... bed side rails up, incontinent of urine....*

By August 3, I was still in Manitoba, would arrive home in two more days. Jean's records for this day described her as having *little affect and talking to herself, slept poorly the previous night.* Jean, now wearing a restraint jacket, her personal care done in bed due to incontinence, is described as *asleep most of day, quiet ... walking in hallways by evening, appearing a little lost ... drowsy affect generally ... found in another's room sleeping on the bed and taken to her own....* She was again put into a restraint jacket. This night she was given 3.75 mg of Imovane, a hypnotic with a pharmacological profile similar to that of benzodiazepines—severe drowsiness and/or impaired coordination are signs of drug intolerance or excessive dosage. Manifestations of rebound insomnia are reported in both sleep lab and clinical studies. The following day, August 4, Jean was described *limping ... bed-seeking, confused and irritable ... speech confused by evening, requires total assist ... near midnight found stripping, attempting to get out of safety jacket, yelling out, incontinent ... physically aggressive to care, scratching and digging fingernails into staff, did not settle once changed.* An injection of loxapine was given Jean at this time for *agitation and aggressiveness.* By 3:00 a.m. Jean was noted: *still awake, putting her legs through rails and calling to be let out ... pt. placed in a Lumex chair and moved to lounge ... has remained awake talking to self for remainder of night ... pt. has stripped herself and removed Attends, pleasant on approach, answering questions appropriately....* By the next day, August 5, Jean lost her balance, slept all morning, *bed-seeks* all afternoon, and was reported as *unable to orient herself or retain information.* By that evening Jean was noted as *wandering in other rooms and refusing to return to her own, telling staff "you can't make me it's my business."* The records indicate that when staff explained others' need for privacy, Jean returned to the nursing station and did not intrude on others.

It is now August 6. Jean was reported as having *asked to go home as she is "not feeling well"… not eating well….* I had just flown back from Winnipeg the night before. A deep ruby red sunset slipping into the ocean as the plane approached for landing. Hot, humid at midnight.

Against Her Will

When I left the province June 8, 1994, Jean was erect, sitting, standing, walking on her own, dressing herself and going to the dining room for meals, required no assistance with her meals. She was continent. By August 6, 1994, she had been in this psychiatric unit for eleven days. I found her, on my return, strapped in a wheelchair, her jaw almost rigid, drooling, unable to sit upright by herself, and incontinent. Her room there was a bare, white cubicle with one window too high to be able to see out. We sat together and I told her where I'd been. As I did, even as I entered her room, her eyes looked at mine with a knowing in them that told me she had been waiting so long, too long, for this acknowledgement. When I told her that I knew about her father and what she had suffered, she wept and told me it was "so hard for her," meaning Jane, her mother, and how "afraid" she (Jean) had been of her father, "to go anywhere with him...." Jean managed to tell me this even with her jaw almost rigid and her speech slurred, and with me passing her Kleenex so she could wipe away the drool coming from her mouth. I went immediately, then, to find the psychiatrist assigned to her, and expressed my shock at her condition and the unfamiliar surroundings, bare of even a chair in her room, windows so high she couldn't see out, in which she has been placed. The psychiatrist's response was, "We aren't running a hotel here. I don't think you would want to take her home and look after her yourself, would you?" This young woman repeated these remarks when I tried to discuss my concerns about the drugs Jean was being given, and told me, "Your mother's brain is destroyed and I would find it acceptable if she had to spend the rest of her life strapped in a wheelchair, if it took that level of medication to control her behaviour." I saw no sign of a "destroyed mind," or spirit, but a person under assault, embattled and trying to come to terms with her life, who was experiencing a poisoning from drugs not given for her benefit or healing, but, it had already been admitted, for the benefit of the system, drugs that prevented her from accessing and using the resources and abilities that lay within her to come to terms with her life, her past, and her natural mortality. The energy of her body and mind forced instead into surviving the toxic onslaught of these imposed drugs, into trying to express, in whatever way she could, the mental and physical pain these drugs were causing her, attempting to exercise her choice to refuse what was harming her. But any possibility of finding and bringing to recall the words she needed was disabled by the toxicity of these same drugs. What recourse had been left to her but to act out her resistance? I remember her words up on Jericho Hill—"I can see it all, I just can't find the words."

Primitive experimenting with the use of psychotropic drugs on a ninety-year-old woman was rationalized, justified, by this so-called need to control behaviour in order to achieve manageability within a system that was not set up to serve and respect people according to their needs, with adequate numbers of staff who are specifically trained for such care. When I continued to express my concern to this psychiatrist that Jean was severely overmedicated, I was told by her that their procedure was "to start with larger doses to see the effect and then work down." I argued that this was an unacceptable approach to take with someone of Jean's age and fragility, reminding her Jean was ninety, and that it went against everything written in the medical literature about the introduction and use of any drug, particularly with persons over sixty, argued unsuccessfully for a reduction in the number of drugs being given to Jean, that these drugs were contributing to Jean's agitation and insomnia. I could find no one who would or could inform me at to Jean's rights at this point, or mine as her representative and trustee, and was reminded that Jean had been admitted involuntarily, which meant, in this psychiatrist's words, that "the unit, we, are absolved of any legal implications related to her treatment." I was not directed to any individual or body, any advocate to whom I could appeal what was being done to Jean. My energy and time was taken up by just being with her in the unit each day to monitor as best I could what was happening to her, to be with her and provide whatever support and encouragement I could in the circumstances, and to speak for her. It was obvious to me that what was being done to Jean here was not for her well-being, but to keep her submissive, deactivated, suppressed.

Later, in 1995–96, when I wrote this hospital's administration to question this lack of information concerning involuntary admissions and appeal processes, their response was that such information "was available in a pamphlet pinned up on a bulletin board in the hospital cafeteria." I had no time to spend in the cafeteria, nor was I ever directed to this source by anyone. There were copies of two signed medical certificates under the Mental Health Act, in Jean's records, one signed by the admitting psychiatrist, another signed by the current psychiatrist with whom I was dealing, that Jean was, in their opinion and as the certificate stated, *mentally disordered and requiring medical treatment in a facility and care, supervision and control in a facility for his own protection or for the protection of others....* And describing Jean thus: *This 90 yr. old female is suffering from severe dementia, her judgement is impaired, and she has no insight ... she can be a danger to others as she has aggressive episodes and she can be a danger to self as she is severely cognitively impaired and not able to look after self. She requires treatment in a hospital, which she refuses. ... admitted to hospital for relevant episodes of aggression and paranoia. Significant cognitive impairment with no insight into her behaviours. Unable to appreciate need for hospitalization. Facility unable to manage her behaviour.* Jean was admitted without her consent on the basis of these opinions expressed by staff at her care facility. She could only be held for fifteen days. After that, another certificate under the Mental Health Act needed to be signed to renew authority for her detention. By August 10, Jean would have been in this unit for fifteen days. There is no certificate covering the period from August 10 until August 24, when another certificate appeared in her records that renewed her detention for the period August 24 until September 8 (she was discharged September 14). The second certificate was signed only by the same young psychiatrist assigned to Jean with whom I had been dealing, who was working under the supervision of a more senior psychiatrist, and gave the following reason for detaining Jean further. *This patient suffers from severe dementia, is aggressive towards others, non-competent with taking her medications, is confused, uncooperative and has no insight into her problem. She requires treatment in hospital as she is dangerous to self and others.*

Over the next several days, my pleas to have the dosages and the numbers of drugs being given Jean reduced were ignored. The psychiatrist assigned to Jean would not consider it. I advised her I wished to take Jean out for a drive, a picnic lunch. Permission was granted for limited periods of time. After our first outing, a drive to the park, Jean was described: *Returned conversant and at times able to carry on appropriate conversation, appears to be less sleepy, pleasant and cooperative during interactions, some preservation of memory, had recollection of conversation in the morning, able to recall events of the morning ....* The drug trazodone was abruptly discontinued, as it had been at the care facility, due to what her records again describe as: *marked postural hypotension,* and was replaced with loxapine as a regular twice-daily dose in addition to the "as needed," referred to in her records as prn, doses she was already receiving. Imovane was replaced with chloral hydrate and alprazolam (Xanax) withdrawn due to what her records stated as: *over sedation.* The severe withdrawal and rebound effects associated with alprazolam (Xanax) were in quick evidence as Jean's mental, emotional, and physical state deteriorated markedly. Insomnia increased. She was reported as *appears to have some visio-spatial difficulties, confusion, restlessness ... unsteady and drowsy ... resistive ... striking out during care, falling asleep during meals....* On August 9, one day before her legal detention in this unit would expire, Jean's records state: *experienced an unwitnessed fall in the hallway....* I was not told of this. I found it later in her records. Later she was described: *verbally intrusive and very angry ... refusing medications, then took the liquid while becoming physically and verbally abusive to staff....* alprazolam (Xanax) was given again, then withheld.

By August 10, Jean was described: *very drowsy, gait unsteady....* That day we went for a picnic lunch to Stanley Park. I brought what I thought were some of Jean's favourite foods—thin-sliced roast beef sandwiches with a little tangy mustard, fresh tomato slices, lemon cake, ice cream and strawberries. And of course tea. We sat near a stream and some cascading willow trees. There were geese napping in a semi-circle around us and Jean threw pieces of her sandwich to the crows. She could not eat much at all and I noticed she had difficulty swallowing. Tea, a little, and some ice cream, a bit of cake, was all she managed. We talked, mostly I did, she listened, nodded, was very quiet, her eyes closed most of the time. My gut knew this could be our last picnic. As I looked down at the untouched food, the strawberries, another August, another memory returning, walking what seems a very long time with my father, a hot afternoon, a park, it feels better under the trees; there are swings, my father pushes me up higher. I like to swing, but not today, I want to go home and lie down. Neither my father nor I know I'm brewing a summer flu. At supper I don't want to eat, tinned carrots too much. My mother says, no dessert strawberries then. Later that night, when it becomes clear I'm sick, she comes with a bowl of strawberries and feeds them to me. I wanted to tell Jean I remembered this, but she was gazing toward the tall cedars across the way from us sighing gently in the breeze off the ocean, and said, uneasily, "maybe we should go now." Back at the hospital parking lot, as I began to help Jean from the car, she cried out in pain. I called a nurse to assist. I had not yet met the gently empathetic woman, also born in Manitoba, near Jean's birthplace, who had just come back on shift and was to be Jean's primary care nurse, who was the one who came, and immediately said, "There must be a lot of pain, she's not a complainer...." Jean was given Tylenol for pain and that evening this nurse wrote: +++*appreciative of care given by writer.*

The next morning alprazolam (Xanax) was again withheld, although given the night before, when Jean was described as *unsteady on her feet and drowsy.* I had requested that I be advised prior to any procedures being considered, or carried out, with regard to Jean, was told after the fact, that a CT scan had been done. Her records stated it *indicates no evidence of metastatic disease ... changes that probably represent ischemic injury.* After the CT scan Jean was given an additional injection of Loxapine, *for agitation.* Her records then indicated: *compliance ...smiles ... pleasant expressions ... restlessness ... confusion ... agitation ... laughing ... pointing finger ... unable to take assistance from staff....* Loxapine was given again *for verbal and physical aggression* and was deemed: *very effective*; Jean reported: *calm and compliant at this time, agreeable to vitals and meds....* after which, it was described, she *bed-seeks,* and seven hours later she became more agitated than ever, at which time she was again given loxapine, *for visual hallucinations and agitation,* her records stated, after which Jean was described: *remains agitated, screamingx2 episodes, speech non-sensical, temperature taken ... requires total assistance and is put to bed for the night.*

At this point, Jean was being given the following drugs daily: Xanax (alprazolam), which had been withdrawn and then reintroduced, with all of the attending withdrawal and rebound effects, as well as loxapine, digoxin, Imovane (which was then replaced by chloral hydrate), two laxatives, Tylenol, and PRN (as needed) doses of loxapine, additional to the daily doses of this neuroleptic already being given to her. I didn't know how to stop what they were doing to my mother, to Jean. Anger had taken over, following it into this vortex of lost control, no boundaries, no protection, feeling overwhelmed and not adequate ... this primal need for a safe place, a mother's arms, smells and tastes of fresh clean air, sounds of the sea, energy, light, warmth, trust, lightness of body and spirit, wind singing the trees, the prairie grasses, could Jean hear, feel any comfort at all? I had begun coming each day in late morning, after staff had completed their morning routines, staying over her lunch time, until Jean would lie down for a rest, and then returning for her late afternoons and suppertimes, staying into the evening until she again lay down to rest. Her primary care nurse from Manitoba had moved her to a room on her own at the east end of the hall, a corner room with lots of light from windows east and south, overlooking trees. Trees and light. I had been able to take Jean for another drive. We picked up muffins and a decaf latte, went to the beach and parked the car. Jean had half a muffin and finished the latte. We even walked a little. Coming back to the hospital, Jean became agitated.

By August 14, Jean's records continued to give witness to a pattern of increasingly aggressive drugging of Jean and of using the consequences of this drugging as a basis for prescribing more drugs and larger dosages. She was described on that day as *wandering the halls asking where she is and how she got here—becoming increasingly restless, frustrated and then agitated, raised her voice while writer tried explaining things to her ... refused meds as offered, striking out at staff, thought form illogical, some word salad, content has paranoid flavour "I know what you want," regular loxapine given* (by injection in her right arm) *... remains awake and agitated, screaming periodically, attempting to climb out of* *bed, verbally and physically aggressive in response* ....Twenty minutes later Jean was given another PRN (as needed) injection of *loxapine for continued agitation* and nurses wrote: *continues to call out and strike out at staff on approach ... remains awake, sitting up in bed picking at bed covers, quiet but verbally aggressive on approach... Jean is noted as asleep around one a.m., awake at 5:00 a.m talking to herself ... affect generally blunted.* By 11:00 a.m. that same morning, when Jean began to again show signs of agitation, she was given another "as needed" dose of loxapine. On this day, Xanax (alprazolam) appeared to have been discontinued. Ten minutes after this most recent dose of loxapine, Jean was described: *posturing++ to right side and assisted to a chair with table top for pt. safety.*

New orders appeared for another drug, Nozinan: *as needed*. An hour later the PRN effect of the loxapine was noted: *effective to reduce agitation and response aggression ... confined to a geri-chair for her own safety because of increased posturing....* The term *posturing* referred to Jean's inability to stand without falling forward or to either side. Her mood was described: *labile, alternating between pleasant and quiet and irritable and threatening....* An hour later, three hours after having been given loxapine, Jean was given her first dose of *as needed* Nozinan. Nozinan is described in the literature as a neuroleptic with strong sedative properties and a potent potentiator of anaesthetics. Central nervous system depression, tachycardia, and orthostatic hypotension are associated with Nozinan. There is also a cautionary warning about using this drug in individuals with glaucoma. Jean refused the Nozinan and her records indicated two staff were "required to squeeze a syringe of the dose into the side of her mouth." Two hours later she was described: *posturing to right, gait unsteady as result of same, assisted into geri-chair for safety. Pt. physically aggressive in response to same.* At this point Jean was given another *as needed* dose of Nozinan (2.5 mg) for: *increased agitation and aggression,* which it was noted: *has little effect, very labile, fluctuating from being smiling and pleasant to being verbally and physically aggressive within seconds ... refused numerous requests to take meds....* Nozinan was then given again one and a half hours after the last dose. Her records indicated Jean refused the additional chloral hydrate, was put into a restraint jacket and placed in bed, which was moved to the lounge for closer observation. It was close to midnight. Jean had partially removed her restraining jacket four times and was attempting to get out of bed.

She was placed in a Lumex chair *for safety*. These heavy recliner-type chairs on wheels hold a person in by their tilt backwards and their tray, which fits on them in the manner of an infant's high-chair food tray. The feeling must have been one of helplessness and entrapment. Jean remained awake in this chair, all night.

The morning of August 16, Jean was *drooling, posturing to the right with an unsteady gait ... kept in geri-chair (Lumex).... Later making her way up and down the halls with same but less severe posturing,* but by noon, described: *physically aggressive in response to care ... put back in geri-chair and moved to a quiet environment....* At this point she was given another what was referred to as an *as needed dose of Nozinan.* After two hours it was noted: *no effect, irritable and physically striking out in response to direction ... labile mood persists with afternoon episodes of sad mood and tearfulness....* What was referred to in Jean's records as PRN, or, *as needed* dosages of drugs are dosages in addition to regular daily prescribed dosages of what was given her. Around 6:00 p.m. that day Jean had a heart attack, A STAT electrocardiogram was done and priority care consulted, after which Jean was given 0.3 mg nitroglycerine. This apparently eased the pain but her pulse remained irregular. It was several days later before I was told, casually, by the same young resident psychiatrist assigned to her with whom I had been dealing, "she had what we think is a heart attack last Tuesday," and that Jean was now wearing a nitroglycerine patch, which would need to be removed for several hours overnight in each twenty-four-hour period to counter toxic buildup of this drug in her system.

The day after Jean's heart attack she was given another *as needed dose* of Nozinan for: *agitation and aggressive behaviour,* replacing loxapine, which had been abruptly withdrawn. She: *begins to drool and posture to the right.* Her mood fluctuated *from pleasant to angry and sad with tearfulness,* within twenty minutes of the drug dose. By noon she was described: *physically aggressive in response to care, confused, refused lunch by throwing same on floor....* little effect from PRN dose of Nozinan. Over the remainder of this day Jean was described: *picking at the air, grabbing out at walls, tables ... pacing ... wandering into rooms ... confused, suspicious of staff ... physically aggressive to care ... assisted into geri-chair, table top applied, patient yelling during same....* A geriatric specialist was called in. Jean was not eating or drinking. She had lost six pounds in one week. He recorded the following: *a differential diagnosis of her agitation includes delirium vs dementia, with pain syndrome/intercurrent illness. Best to avoid benzodiazapines ... relatively new onset of bilateral pleural effusion....* This geriatric specialist ordered testing of the pleural effusion, i.e., fluid building up around Jean's lungs. At this point, the resident psychiatrist noted: *marked side effects from Nozinan, ++aggression, plan is to increase Nozinan....* This pattern continued in the following days. A description of what was termed a *good effect* from a dose of Nozinan was described as *no agitation or aggression with care ... mood labile, affectionate @ times, kissing writer on the cheek, also calling out for help, other times appears distraught with head on table covered with hands. Affect full range, congruent, speech irrelevant ... appears to be having visual hallucinations, pointing and picking at the air, poor eye contact....*

Pieces of Voice

Jean's records continued to describe her as *labile ... resistive.. hostile, screaming and hitting out, picking at the air and having a conversation with no one but becoming ++hostile when interrupted ... becoming more spontaneously agitated with contact.* But I had never seen any of this behaviour at any time when I was with her. What I did see was Jean's marked physical deterioration, extreme fatigue, inability to hold herself upright, inability to swallow, her expressions of pain, her incontinence, her loss of function generally, her frequent expressions, "I don't know where to go ... how to run, where home is...." Nozinan was being given more frequently and in increasingly larger doses and Jean was spending more and more time in the geri-chair, where she usually was when I came in to be with her, or lying down on her bed. She was described by staff as: *lurching and unsteady on her feet, pt. complains to nurses of "not feeling too good"... mood lability escalating ... screams and swears when staff attempt care, direction, meds ... frequently asks about "home," wants to leave hospital ... telling staff she is "going home and doesn't know where that is or where she is now," observed standing in front of an empty chair, gesturing and talking loudly. Could not state whether she saw someone there … remains awake sitting up in bed, talking occasionally as if someone was in the room. Asking them to get out and leave her alone.* After this Jean then slept for the rest of the night, having refused to take chloral hydrate earlier that evening. The following evening, a note indicated that, when she struck out at staff on their approach she apologized. She refused chloral hydrate again, and was given another dose of Nozinan. In her records it was noted that with my visits there was: *reduction in her labile mood and an increase in the range of her affect.*

Jean was not agitated or reactive with me at any time. I spoke to her as if she could understand me and asked her what she would like to do, trying to, at least with me, preserve as much choice for her as possible. Her long-term memories had been a rich source of communication, connection between us. I spoke with her also of current things, to which she also responded. However, her ability to swallow and speak had by now been impaired and it required an effort for her to drink, eat, and talk. I had put an album together, of photos I had taken while away. We turned the pages often, moving from images of Jane's childhood home in Scotland, to Jean's childhood in Manitoba; photos of the abandoned farm, which I felt could be disturbing for Jean, were absent, and instead there were those fields running to sky that surrounded the town, where Jean had walked, ridden Sam the horse, a vista so wide, as I stood at an edge of town looking toward the abandoned farm, I needed several camera shots to capture a sense of it. When I held up the three photos together to show the panoramic spread of fields, horizon, sky, Jean nodded immediately. "Yes," she said, and looked away. Trees had been a surprise, coming in off that prairie heat into town, tall elms, deep and dark, a cool refuge. Jane's little house her sons bought for her in town, still there somewhere nearby, but I was unable to find it. There were some pictures of her mother Jane, herself as a child, her brothers, one of myself with her, from my childhood in that little village, and the house we lived in there, still standing. I had found the cabins where we stayed at West Hawk Lake, updated somewhat, neat grass and plants in containers and window boxes, but something in me knew them, for what they had been. The dock, where Jean and I lay in the sun, was gone. A sign by the lake now told the story of how it came to be different than other lakes in this Precambrian Shield; circular, and very deep, from a fiery birth, an inter-planetary body striking earth one hundred million years ago. What memories the images in these photos or my memories evoked for Jean she did not express. She listened, nodded, was mostly quiet, and sad. There were times when an expression came into her eyes as though she was perplexed or confused by what I was describing of her past, mine, that I came to understand as part of her sadness, that she had other perspectives, her own experiences of those memories, but had become too weak, too sick, too overwhelmed by drugs to be able to speak of them, or to relate them to what she was seeing.

One afternoon, when we were sitting in the dining lounge, a man came in and joined us at our table. He was soft-spoken, and told us he had been in the air force and was stationed near Brandon, Manitoba, and in Winnipeg, during the war. He talked a little, Jean responded, smiled, recognized the location. She had worked for the air force during the war, and Camp Shilo, the army station where my father taught, was in the vicinity of Brandon. I hoped there would be a familiar connection with this gentleman who had just come into the unit. When we were returning to Jean's room after, she said, clearly, "That was a nice conversation." I wondered, again, on what basis the psychiatrist had concluded Jean's "mind was destroyed."

By August 24, Jean was described: *posturing forward with her hand on the small of her back, and confined to a geri-chair. Swings her fists at staff.* By now Jean was receiving 7.5 mg of Nozinan three times daily and additional PRN (as needed) doses, which, on this day, were given to Jean at 11:30 a.m. and 1:45 p.m. with what was stated as *no effect,* but in fact, her records immediately after these additional dosages described *increased agitation, hitting out whenever staff approach, speech slurred and nonsensical...* When the psychiatrist was paged she increased the regular dose of Nozinan from 7.5 to 10 mg three times daily, and the individual PRN (as needed) dosages from 2.5 to 5 mg. At this point Jean was injected with another *as needed* dose at the increased level of 5mg at 3:10 p.m., this one at almost twice the dosage, within four and a half hours, in addition to the regular daily dosages of 7.5 mg three times daily, now increased to 10 mg. Staff then confined Jean to a wheelchair. Forty minutes later Jean was described: *calling out loudly, speech confused and irrelevant, suspicious, disoriented to place and time, some agitated episodes and angry gestures ... nourishment offered but patient spilled it to floor ... limited effect of previous PRN dose, regular dose Nozinan refused* (it appeared to have then been given by injection)

... refused supper ... threw the rest to floor, became agitated and calling out loudly and waving arms when nurse tried to feed her... Another PRN (as needed) dose of Nozinan at 5.0 mg was given approximately three hours after the regular dose was administered.

On the same day, August 24, this psychiatrist signed another certificate under the Mental Health Act to detain Jean for an additional two weeks. The certificate contained no indication of treatment, no mention of Jean's age, no second opinions required or offered. At this point Jean was suffering withdrawal from loxapine and particularly Xanax (alprazolam). Yet, in this withdrawal period it was perceived that Jean's behaviour, so-called, was not being controlled by the newly introduced replacement neuroleptic, Nozinan, and the dosage of this drug was markedly increased. After this intensive and repeated drugging with Nozinon, Jean was reported with insomnia overnight, *and drowsy and unsteady on her feet and posturing forward* in the morning. She was put in a wheelchair with restraining strap. At 11:45 a.m., in spite of the geriatric specialist's warning not to use any more benzodiazepine, Jean was given 2 mg of Ativan, to ensure *compliance for pleural-centesis,* a procedure whereby a needle was used to penetrate between the ribs and a sample of fluid from around the lungs drawn off to be examined for what type of cells were present, including those that would indicate metastasized breast cancer. Jean was reported: *asleep shortly after, throughout the procedure and very difficult to arouse.*

In fact she remained drugged, and by 8:00 p.m. had barely opened her eyes for brief periods of time and could not hold her upper body erect in the geri-chair. Her records indicate she *requires constant repositioning in geri-chair ... took ½ hour to feed ... slightly resistive ... limbs too weak to move, fell asleep immediately after feeding ... Nozinan is withheld due to drowsiness....* Jean remained in this condition for seventy-two hours after receiving the Ativan, and is described: *requires verbal directions to open her eyes, speech slurred, drooling heavily and some difficulty noted swallowing....* She was unable to recognize me. By noon August 27, nurses indicated *escalating agitation; patient irritable and hostile, striking out on approach. Confused and non-sensical. Picking at the air. Does not recognize her daughter. Refusing lunch....* At this point another dose (10 mg) of Nozinan was given to Jean, who was still unable to walk or support herself, and remained in her chair. By 2:00 p.m. Jean was described with: *escalating agitation, physically aggressive on all contact,* and an additional PRN dose of Nozinan was given. By 5:00 p.m. that same day Jean was having abdominal pain and her pulse was irregular. She was given Tylenol. She did not eat supper, was not able to be aroused for any nourishment in the evening or overnight. Episodes of anxiety were recorded, Jean stating "I don't know where to go or what to do." She had been expressing this with me as well. It would become a recurring theme. Her eyelids drooped now, her swallowing more difficult. I was feeding her both lunch and supper. It took an a hour or more. Her autonomic reflexes were noticeably impaired. Neuroleptic-induced neurological disorders involving spasms can affect any voluntary muscle, including those involved with speech, swallowing, and breathing, as well as gait. Jean was now having episodes of aspirating her food and drink. We had to go very slowly. She no longer seemed to be fully conscious. After lunch, I would try to lie her down for a rest, " I don't know where to go, what to do, where's home...?" a constant refrain from then on. I found a note in Jean's records: *found by nurses putting dirt and leaves in her mouth. Immediately removed same when told to. Stated "it probably wasn't a good idea."*

At this point Jean could no longer walk down the hall any distance; she was, she told me, too tired. Her shoulder was noted as having: *evident old bruising,* presumably this suggested her shoulder may have been injured in a fall on this ward. She was sent for an x-ray, which she refused, and was given an *as needed* dose of Nozinan. Meanwhile the results of the pleural-centesis had come back, stating: *the cells are too degenerate to allow proper interpretation ... this is an unsatisfactory specimen, the amount submitted is small and the specimen shows marked degenerative changes.* Was the specimen collected improperly, held too long before testing? I was told the results were inconclusive, the cells too old to tell if they were malignant or not. The suspicion of metastasis of her breast cancer was suggested to me and that further aggressive or invasive investigations of this were considered inappropriate in Jean's circumstances. In her records there was an unsigned form for "surgical and treatment consent," with a note written on it: *see involuntary consent signed by Dr — .* This individual, noted as the VP of Medicine, had signed the forms for Jean's involuntary detention in the psychiatric unit and her involuntary treatment, which was described as: *medical and psychological treatment as clinically indicated and prescribed by hospital medical staff.* Once someone was involuntarily admitted to such a unit, anything could be done that was deemed in their best interest. The whole point of Jean's detention was for the best interest of the health care system, and, in my opinion, at this juncture, in the interest of experimentation with neuroleptic pharmacology. My agreeing, or not, to whatever procedures were done to Jean were irrelevant. They would do them anyway.

At the end of August, Jean asked me, "Is this Wednesday?" It was. She was walking again, but clutching at her back and grimacing in pain as she walked. In her records she was described as appearing tired, pacing the hall *posturing forward, irritable on approach, doesn't want to talk to anybody ... threw her medication at staff, stating "get out of here, go away" and attempting to kick staff....* After which she received another 5-mg as needed dose of Nozinan. When this only increased Jean's agitation she was given chloral hydrate two hours later, at midnight, as an as needed dose, increased from 500 mg to 1 gram, after which she remained awake all night (250 mg is considered by pharmacological literature to be a "safe" dose for those over sixty years). This continuing pattern of increased use of drugs at higher doses to control the toxic effects they produced was accompanied by the predictable, increasingly toxic reactions which were evident in Jean. When Jean became sedated and unable to walk or strike out, in other words helpless and submissive, the drug dose was referred to in her records as having *good effect*. When drug toxicity then produced in Jean attendant symptoms of agitation, anger, hallucinations etc., the drug was said to have *no effect*. A strange and carefully worded lexicon.

August 30, 1994—two years ago our golden retriever, Sam, had died, fluid drowning her lungs. That night I had a dream, in which I am looking down on the open back end of what seems to be a moving van, looking at Sam standing in a cardboard packing box as the truck's doors slide shut, saying to myself, " I can't do this." I see Sam get out of the box and start coming out of the truck, then going back in and climbing back into the box, and I realize she wants to go... Was it always to be loss, hers and mine, just finding my mother, having to let her go?

Where's Home?

It was September. Jean was being given Tylenol for frequent episodes of pain throughout her body. Psychiatric nursing staff now believed that Jean's so-called *unprovoked aggression* and what that term implied was, rather, a pain *response* to being touched and moved by staff as they cared for her. Staff were beginning to talk more about her pain, and the pain in terms of *her* metastasis. No mention was ever made about painful musculo-skeletal effects of neuroleptics and of course there was never any suggestion that Jean had been subjected to aggression, was responding *to* aggression. At this time, Jean was again given 1 gr of chloral hydrate and subsequently showed signs of heavy sedation. On September 5, she was described as *verbally aggressive ... noted to be ++sedated, posturing forward, drooling, scissor gait, speech slurred and illogical, required spoonfeeding for lunch....* Her vitals were all depressed: temperature, pulse, respiration, and blood pressure. A later entry in her records, referring to 9:00 a.m. that morning, indicated: *put self on the floor following breakfast.* I was told this later on that day and requested that she be seen by a doctor immediately (according to her records it appeared that Jean had fallen on a couple of occasions prior, but I was never told of those incidents). The head of this psychiatry unit happened to be in the building. He discontinued the chloral hydrate being given to Jean *as needed,* which was a 1,000-mg dose, to be followed up by another 500-mg dose, *if the first one is not effective.* This doctor was never in contact with me. I had been trying to get this chloral hydrate discontinued, but the resident psychiatrist had flatly refused. She "wanted Jean to have at least six hours sleep every night," disregarding warnings in pharmaceutical literature: *Central nervous system effects from this drug include: nightmares, headache, confusion and malaise, as well as paradoxical and idiosyncratic effects, among which are hallucinations, delirium, unusual excitement, disorientation, incoherence and paranoia. Recommended dose for those over 60 is half the adult dose, or 250 mg....* This psychiatrist had also been steadily increasing the dose of Nozinan given to Jean to 40 mg a day plus *as needed* doses at 5 mg each. At this time of Jean's fall, the director of the unit had also reduced this amount of Nozinan being given her. Jean's records indicated the discontinuation of chloral hydrate was only temporary; it would be given again.

Pain in all parts of Jean's body, particularly her back, continued to be increasingly evident, along with her difficulty with walking, her unsteady gait. Her eyes remained closed most of the time I was with her, her swallowing compromised, her eating laboriously slow. Nozinan continued to be given in 5-mg doses *as needed,* as well as regular doses three times daily. Tylenol was replaced with morphine sulphate. Once nursing staff in this psychiatric unit became aware of pain as the significant factor in Jean's reaction to being touched, moved, by care staff, her reaction was referred to as *response aggression,* rather than *unprovoked aggression.* Nursing staff communicated this to the psychiatrist, who in turn told me that once morphine doses became established, Jean would be discharged, that "others need her bed." She suggested that "morphine would increasingly be the drug of choice to be used to "manage" Jean, as what was "likely a metastatic process continues." In other words, the anti-psychotic drugs would be quietly phased out. A care plan for Jean that reflected this changed assessment of her had been prepared by her primary care nurse in the psychiatric unit, who had been helpful and empathetic, but who would soon be leaving to return to Manitoba. She had taken this plan to a meeting with the care facility nursing staff who had initiated Jean's involuntary admission to the psychiatric unit, to discuss Jean's care needs with them, a specific plan for them to follow once she became resident there again, on her discharge from the unit. After that meeting, she warned me that this care facility was "not a good place for Jean." I felt her warning deeply, and my fear that there would be no place for Jean. I could only hope the facility had received some guidance and a better perspective from this nurse regarding Jean's state of health and her essential care needs. I had planned to seek a transfer to a more quiet, care-oriented residence for her, had no idea how long that would take, and in the meantime, whenever she was discharged from this unit, would watch, like a hawk, her care at the facility to which, at that point, she would have to return. I knew I was already exhausted and there seemed to be no one within the system to whom I could turn, to be an advocate for Jean. Feeling very much alone in this, I had no idea what lay ahead, what conditions would meet us, as Jean returned to a care facility that, it had been made clear, didn't want her.

During these last days in the geriatric psychiatry unit, Jean was placed in a restraint jacket at night with bed rails up. On one occasion, when her legs became entrapped in the railings, Jean became angry when a nurse tried to help, then apologized when disentangled, and said, "I know it's not your fault, you're only helping," and told the nurse it was because she was "very tired and needing to sleep." She requested only one side rail be left up. As more extra Nozinan was given for various episodes of what was referred to as *agitation,* Jean became more obviously lethargic, and affected in motor control. She was described as *pale and appearing very tired.* Pain all over her body was becoming more and more marked. Morphine was withheld *due to drowsiness.* Nozinan, *as needed,* was then said to be given to *promote relaxation and sleep.* Jean had begun coughing, was observed placing her cup in her food. She was telling me her legs pained her. She wanted to walk but became tired after a few steps and couldn't go on.

It was September 10, a Saturday night. Jean was still in the psychiatry unit, once again past the legal period of her detention. A beautiful crisp September evening. The sun had not yet set and lit up the trees. I wrapped Jean up in her coat and took her outside the hospital in a wheelchair. We were under a young tree and in the sunlight. It was chillier than I anticipated. Spine and rib cage clouds lay like bones across an arc of sky. Jean was silent, did not smile, a look of sadness in her eyes, her face when she looked at me as I talked about the warmth of the sun in the chill of the air. A look of disappointment, of knowing, that she was dying, that she would not come back from this, was what I saw there. Many feelings collided in me, grief at the disappointment I saw in her look, anger at what had happened to her, my own inability to make it better, I wanted so much to make it better for her. Once back on the unit, Jean had intermittent pain in her feet, legs, and back. She was very tired, but when she lay down, she became anxious and agitated. Her husband, she asked for him, told me, "He's here," holding her arms out and then clasping her chest. She asked me about her mother, her brothers, "Where are they now?" That she was the only one left of her family, Jean said, "It is a shock," and spoke of something lost, or "He lost it." She became upset, wanted to go home and I didn't know what she meant by home. "How do I get there," she would ask me, over and over. "I don't know how to go, I don't know where to run," she would say many times. How could I ease her heart? except to say, "Home is your heart, stay in your heart," and told her I was there with her.

I thought later, of when Jean, my father and I were together, my memories of our Sunday afternoon drives, when he was home, and trips, to West Hawk, leaving those rooms on Osborne Street, the street, the city behind, moving through a changing landscape, to pastures, grazing cows, and then that other world of emerging rock, tree, lake, sky, the surprise of it, the first time, those bulrushes sighing and rustling in ditches, lily pads floating in ponds the colour of my mother's strong tea, a world existing in parallel to Osborne Street that I had not known until then. Another journey. I am four, Jean my young mother. We are with my father in the car. I am watching telephone poles from the floor of the back seat of the car, wondering when we will *be there*. It would be a long trip, across Canada to a conference for teachers in Quebec City. The small child remembers uncles and aunts, a scary rooster, my father leaping out of my uncle's house and into our car, after I had released the gearshift. There was a hill. My father's brother was like him, slight of build. My mother's brother very tall. He was a professor at an agricultural college. They had a little dog, and chickens out behind their very large brick house. There were two sons, cousins of mine, who were already big men; the younger son, Jean's nephew, would go missing with his plane during the war that was coming. I was left with friends in Montreal. I remember eating a lot of oatmeal there, and feeling abandoned, until my parents returned from Quebec City. There was a ferry ride to a place called Newfoundland, and I was very hungry the whole time. I didn't like fish. At the World's Fair in New York, I only remember looking down from somewhere very high, seeing what looked like a miniature village lit up. It looked so very far away, and made me feel uneasy. In photos from that time, Jean looked happy, at ease. My father's photos, there are very few, hard to read. I remember him as quiet, gentle with me, kind. I felt comfortable with him. In those photos I looked well scrubbed, dressed up, and not liking it much. I have never liked having my picture taken.

By morning Jean was unable to walk and was placed in a wheelchair with a restraining belt. She was now being given Losec, because her red blood cell count had dropped and it was suspected she was bleeding internally ... Losec is used to treat duodenal ulcer. Some of the adverse effects accompanying this drug use are: *dizziness, pareasthesia, somnolence, insomnia, vertigo, mental confusion, agitation, depression and hallucination, particularly in severely ill patients.* Also noted are: *angioedema, fever and bronchospasm, increased sweating, peripheral edema, blurred vision and taste perversion.*

When I fed her lunch and supper, which were taking between one and two hours, I was asked to give her oral doses of Nozinan and morphine mixed in with her food. I complied with this request, but with a painfully divided heart, wanting to break us both out of there, no more drugs, no more abuse. Jean had upper chest and eye pain. Her feet, legs, hands, and arms had begun to swell. Alarmed, I removed her wedding band. On Monday morning, September 12, in spite of my arguing against it, Jean was booked to undergo an x-ray series of her GI tract, which would involve sedation, again with Ativan. I argued that, given Jean's already heavily sedated state, the dangerous level of sedation Jean experienced previously with Ativan, and her disabled swallowing reflex, I did not believe this to be safe for her, or even possible, and requested only monitoring of her red blood count be done, since she was already on Losec to treat the duodenal bleed. "We have to do it," her resident psychiatrist told me. Jean's records indicated that a geriatric specialist, called in after Jean had a heart attack on August 16, recommended that benzodiazepines, Ativan being one of this class, not be given to Jean. When I protested, the psychiatrist insisted she had "no alternative, since Jean might be haemorrhaging internally and we need to find out where." I realized how few within this system had the honesty, humility, the courage to act in Jean's best interest rather than for their own self-protection, and to cover their ignorance.

I came to the unit early the next morning to try, again, to convince them to stop the procedure. The psychiatrist I spoke with at the nursing desk was not Jean's, and looked at me as though I was another customer for the unit. Jean was sedated with Ativan and taken down for the barium swallow. I prayed she would refuse this. She did. She was reported as *non-compliant to the procedure.* My discussion with the psychiatrist regarding the harmfulness to Jean of this procedure is recorded in her notes in Jean's records as: *daughter agrees.* For the rest of this day Jean was described, not surprisingly, as *sedated and compliant to all procedures ... becomes breathless ... Nozinan 10mg p.o. and morphine sulphate 2mg. p.o. withheld as patient++drowsy.* That evening, at 9:00 p.m. *1000 mg. chloral hydrate given as patient wide awake.* Two hours later another 500 mg chloral hydrate again given for sleeplessness. The maximum safe dosage of chloral hydrate for those over sixty is 250 mg.

The next morning, September 13, Jean was noted: *not opening her eyes ... requiring assistance to ambulate ... continues drowsy and not opening her eyes during conversation, clutching at arms and chest, tearful and appearing distressed, saying, "my arms hurt" ... Dr. notified and staggered dose of morphine given early as per Dr.'s instructions, vitals within normal range.* Jean remained confined to a geri-chair over the afternoon and was observed: *emotionally labile between quick angry swearing bouts and pleasant warm interactions ... edema evident both lower legs ankles and feet ... appears only to be oriented to her own name and her daughter's name ... that evening: placed in bed with restraint jacket, refusing oral meds ... remains awake until 2:30 a.m....* She was discharged from this unit the following day.

Jean, We Hardly Knew You

September 14, the day of her discharge from this unit, Jean was recorded as: *drowsy and complaining "it hurts" ... respiration moist ... ++unsteady on feet, needing assistance to stand and only able to take a few steps, two-staff assist to geri-chair ... continues to complain of pain but unable to elaborate ... left ward with daughter, personal belongings and discharge package sent with patient. Affect bright....* Affect bright? Jean, we hardly knew you.... As Jean and I left the psychiatry unit, Jean strapped in a wheelchair, unable to keep her upper body upright, her hands, legs, feet swollen with edema and only able to wear large slippers on her feet, we passed the reception desk. No one was there except the ward receptionist. She said goodbye to Jean with tears in her eyes.

Nursing assessments of Jean at her discharge from this psychiatry unit stated that she was *verbally and physically resistive to care with response aggression ... she voiced no thoughts of self-harm although occasionally sad ...consistently disoriented x2 or more spheres and displayed no psychotic features....* The psychiatrist who was assigned to Jean wrote in her discharge report that Jean was experiencing *multi-*

175

infarct dementia complicated by behavioural problems with paranoid and schizoid personality traits, probably had such elements in her personality before the onset of multi-infarct dementia five years ago. This was not a profile of Jean, her personality, her character, but of the effects of drugs given her. This psychiatrist's description of the drugs imposed on Jean stated: *during the course in hospital it was noticed that she is extremely sensitive to medication and to any changes in medication....* At a meeting about Jean's discharge, this psychiatrist fed back to me, and to others in attendance, what I had said all along about my mother Jean, and the effect these drugs were having on her, as though my words were her own. She no longer spoke of "controlling Jean's behaviour" but of Jean as "someone exquisitely sensitive to medication and we have to settle for most of the aggression controlled if we can maintain her normal walking, eating, sitting etc...." It would seem this psychiatric doctor had not noticed that Jean could no longer walk, sit, stand, or eat, since coming into this psychiatric unit.

As Jean and I were preparing to leave the unit and return to her care facility, we were given a discharge packet to take with us, in it a file labelled, "Personal and Family History." I read this while sitting on Jean's bed, having removed it from the packet. Since I was the only one to provide any history to the psychiatric social worker, who had prepared this report, I saw how, once again, my attempts to give some understanding of Jean's independent and private life were translated into another profile to justify what was done to Jean. It was a mistake to think it would be helpful to Jean, to tell the psychiatric social worker that she had undergone trauma in childhood with an alcoholic and abusive father. I saw how this invasion of her privacy was used to generate a profile of Jean in accordance with the pathologizing labels used by the psychiatrist in her discharge summary, *an abnormal personality—schizoid and paranoid.* At one point, in the psychiatric social worker's report, Jean was described as a person *who did not discuss her thoughts and feelings with others and could be extremely critical and short-tempered ... a driven woman in her quest for independence and autonomy ... she did not have friends or seek out the company of others....* An interview with me of under an hour, about ninety years of Jean's life, produced a string of conjectures about what I said, and didn't say, or even had knowledge of, with a focus on negative *possibilities* that were written into records that became Jean, how she was perceived and approached. I immediately drew this to the attention of the psychiatric social worker. Her response was to blame the "transcription of her remarks made at general rounds, that these then passed into the records." The report, which had already been presented at general rounds in this hospital, also stated: *Jean left her husband and moved to Winnipeg when her daughter was five years old.* Jean and I left in the spring of 1940 for Winnipeg, where Jean obtained office work and my father joined us after the school year ended. The above are just two examples of what ran through the whole report. My naivety about leading questions and saying "I don't know" left Jean's life open to interpretation and being constructed to fit a "diagnosis" that was being imposed on her. Jean's *discharge package* under my arm, we left, back to the care facility.

The Swimmer Swims Beyond Them Far Out to Sea

When Jean and I entered the care facility, it felt a surreal world. No one greeted us. No one welcomed Jean back. Our presence, unacknowledged, we were ghosts, unseen, it seemed. Care aides were silent. Once in her room, and as Jean sat strapped to a chair because she could no longer hold herself upright, her hands, face, legs, and arms swollen to an alarming size, the nurse who had previously been the acting director and who initiated Jean's involuntary committal to the psychiatric unit finally appeared. I let her know I would be on hand, each day and all day to support Jean's care for as long as necessary. I did not say I had no idea how Jean and I would get through even the next hour. But the nurse was here to tell us that she was now in charge of what she referred to as much more extensive and ongoing renovations to the facility, some of which had been in progress over the past several months, including alterations to areas adjacent to residents' rooms, Jean's in particular. The facility's former administrator had resigned during Jean's detainment in the psychiatric unit and was replaced by an administrator who now was also temporary director of care, taking over from this nurse, who was now preoccupied with plans of reorganization which fully engaged her time. Jean's *ongoing care plan*, prepared by the psychiatric unit and discussed at a care conference prior to Jean's discharge from the unit, which was to have been printed out and placed above Jean's bed here at the facility for all care staff to refer to, she said, was not in place, but she was "working on it." It would not appear while Jean was in the facility, although it would later be claimed, to an investigator, that it was posted in plain sight over Jean's bed for all staff to see. I was told the staff nurse at the facility to whom the care plan was given, when met with by the psychiatric unit, would not be in the facility until her night shift, later that evening.

A part of Jean's care plan was that she have meals in her room, which I would be feeding her. Lunch and supper that day were brought to Jean's room, an hour to an hour and a half after the meals had been served in the dining room and I had to ask care aides passing by the room to bring her something to eat. But by the time any food arrived, Jean had already received morphine and was too sedated to eat anything. The food was unpalatable and inappropriate for her needs, served in white Styrofoam containers, "in case she brought anything infectious back with her."

Jean was restless, feverish, and trying to move, but couldn't support herself, kept falling forward like a rag doll and, if not strapped in, would fall right out of her chair. Her eyes, for the most part, were closed. I was afraid to leave her alone. She didn't speak, seemed to me to be semi-conscious. When nursing staff came to give Jean her noon and 6:00 p.m. morphine, I explained my concern that Jean's edema was worsening, spreading from her legs, feet, arms, and hands to her body and face, and that her pain did not appear to be managed by the morphine levels she was being given. No one came back to check on her, except a care aide, once, to ask if she needed "a diaper change." The staff nurse familiarized with Jean's care needs, checked in with us when she came on shift, and again, once, during the evening. The night of September 14, Jean's first night back in the facility, their records note: *resident appears to be in a lot of pain*. A further note indicates: *not yet treated for possible scabies due to allergic and poss. agitation at this time*. This would have involved complete body covering with an insecticidal agent, permethrin, spraying Raid around her room, and removing all of her clothing for sterilization.

September 15, 1994—Jean's second day back in this facility. I had gone home around ten o'clock the previous night and arrived that morning around 8:00 a.m. A care aide was assisting Jean with personal care. Jean appeared delirious, restless, and in pain. She was quiet, very weak, and unable to move without help, but restlessly trying to move herself. It was 11:00 a.m. when I noticed the nitroglycerine patch, still on from 8:00 a.m. yesterday. I notified the staff nurse. There was no record of the patch having been removed. He came into Jean's room, and without speaking to Jean or myself, pulled the patch off Jean's chest without comment or any kind of check of Jean, who had been groaning and saying she had a "terrible pain in her head." This pain is one of the symptoms of nitroglycerine toxicity, which occurs when such nitro-patches are not removed for eight to ten hours during each twenty-four-hour period. I requested Jean be seen by her doctor as soon as possible. Still no one came to assist us, or even ask if there was anything needed. I was not able to bear Jean's full weight on my own. Care aides walked past the door. At this point I realized we were being ignored, given a message that Jean was not wanted here.

Later in the afternoon I tried, briefly, to leave Jean alone in her room in order to find a care aide who could come and help me put her to bed, as she continued restless, feverish, and in distress, falling forward almost into her own lap even when tied into her chair with a cloth belt, but wanting and trying to keep moving anyway. Ignored by staff, I returned to check on Jean, found her on her hands and knees on the floor with her head up against her bed. I asked a nurse to come to help me, who, when she saw Jean on her knees, said she would call a care aide to help me, then said "maybe in the meantime she'll get up by herself." I asked this same nurse if Jean could have her morphine just at the end of her supper, so she could eat something before sedation, told her I didn't think the morphine dosages were controlling Jean's pain, assuming she would let Jean's doctor know. Instead she became argumentative. Jean's supper did not arrive until 6:30 p.m., a full hour and a half after it was served in the dining-room. Jean's morphine dose was now half an hour overdue; Jean was in obvious physical distress. At 6:45 p.m. I asked a care aide passing by in the hallway to notify this nurse of Jean's situation. I was in tears. By this time I could not hold them back. As I sat beside Jean and told her I was sorry, she said to me, "Go, just go." I told her I wouldn't go, that I wanted to stay with her, and would. The care aide returned with a message from the nurse saying, "She is on her supper break and will come up and give Jean her morphine at 7:00 p.m., when supper break is over." When this nurse finally appeared, I told her that Jean's morphine to manage her pain was now an hour late; her only comment was, "I thought you wanted it given after her supper." An hour after this incident, about 8:00 p.m., Jean's doctor did finally come to see her. It did not appear he had maintained any contact with her once she was taken to the psychiatry unit. His immediate reaction upon seeing Jean was shock and consternation. He examined her, told me she was very ill, with not long to live, that fluid could be taken off her lungs, easing her heart, but it would return. He ordered all drugs, including digoxin, be stopped, except for a diuretic and some antibiotic, along with morphine sulphate to control her pain. I remained grateful for this doctor's humane, warm, and friendly relationship with Jean and the quality of life he now attempted to provide for her at the end of her life. His only rebuke to the above nurse was to say to her, referring to Jean, "She's very ill."

In 1995, when I was reviewing Jean's records for the first time, prior to requesting an investigation of her treatment, I found this nurse's report, her version of the above events: *resident weepy, weak on legs, uncooperative and aggressive at times. Edema persists both lower extremities ... appetite poor, fluids encouraged. Daughter in visiting all evening* (I had been there since 8:00 a.m., and constantly. There was no aggression or agitation). Referring to myself, she wrote: *weepy, crying and demanding of care from care staff.* I had broken into tears trying to explain Jean's serious condition to a care aide when this nurse was on supper break. *Explanations given re: care and reassured. Appears calmer after speaking with Dr,.* and that she *has explained to the care aides that Mrs. Muir is very stressed so that's why she is behaving this way.* In the aftermath of an investigation by provincial ministry of health personnel, a representative of the Registered Nurses Association of BC indicated that the facility had verbally reprimanded this nurse, but because, in their words, the problem is systemic, there will be no formal discipline.

What is referred to as a *serious incident report* also appeared in Jean's records for that morning of September 15, fifteen hours prior to her doctor finding her in a critically ill state on the evening of September 15, and thirteen days before she died. The nurse who wakened Jean and attempted to give her morphine medication wrote in this report *Jean grabbed my throat and attempted to choke me ... I calmly and quickly removed her hand from my throat, calmly spoke to her, did not encourage medication at that time, removed myself from the room, completed the appropriate documentation, as of this time no bruising to my neck—no residual damage other than scaring me to pieces!!! —very sudden aggression on Jean's part.* This registered nurse's responsibility to recognize Jean was in serious medical distress at the time was not acknowledged, nor that she did not notice, or check that Jean's nitroglycerine patch had been on for almost twenty-four hours rather than the maximum of ten hours, and that Jean was delirious and in pain, that edema was increasing all over her body. None of this was included in this RN's report, nor was Jean's doctor notified, nor her condition monitored. All the report states as a follow-up was: *the employee is in satisfactory condition, shaken up but no injuries.* Nothing concerning Jean nor how this nurse approached Jean, a resident in her care, when she wakened her. Again Jean's records presented Jean as the problem and indicated neglect of her medical distress.

Jean was transferred the next morning to the emergency ward of a nearby hospital. Paramedics who came to transport Jean entered her room like furniture movers, noisy and jocular. When I asked them to keep their voices down, they did respond, becoming gentler with her. The new administrator/acting director of care, who had never come anywhere near us until this moment, appeared as Jean was being wheeled out of her room and attempted to hug me. No one else appeared. No one spoke to us on the way out. No one appeared to know, or care to know how ill Jean was. I will never forget how helpless, how hurt, how angry and distraught I was at the hell Jean was going through.

I rode over in the ambulance with Jean. She was very quiet. One of the paramedics rode in back with us. Perhaps by then he had put a face to Jean—his grandmother, somebody's mother, his manner and tone gentler, more reassuring, more respectful of her presence, her awareness. We remained on the emergency ward from 9:00 a.m. to 6:00 p.m., until a bed was found for Jean on the medical ward. Emergency staff appeared tense, annoyed, even hostile in some cases to the both of us. By now my tears just kept coming and I could not stop them. They refused my presence while they examined Jean. Although her eyes remained closed and she did not speak, she became agitated and cried out when they attempt to touch her or move her in anyway. They wanted to start an IV. I overheard them deciding to inject her with loxapine. Outrage at the complete lack of insight and compassion toward Jean that I had been witnessing for too long impelled me to confront these doctors and nurses. They will NOT give Jean loxapine, I said, and told them why. Perhaps it was a look in my eye, tone in my voice that made them back off. There was no further problem when I explained to Jean what was being done and why. It was clear staff wanted me to leave, but I stayed, holding Jean's hand while they took blood, put in IV, did other examinations, then left us alone. It was now past supper time. I asked for some nourishment for Jean. When it arrived and as I was about to help Jean with some supper, she was transferred upstairs to the medical ward.

Once on the medical ward, Jean received a visit from the geriatric specialist who had seen Jean when she was on the psychiatry ward. One would expect a specialist in geriatrics would demonstrate more human insight than this particular physician did as he stood at Jean's bedside and began to talk to me across her, about an increase in fluid on her lungs and the carcinoma he suspected, and its prognosis. I had begun signalling him to stop talking in front of Jean, at which point he paused and said with obvious irritation, "She won't understand any of this." By this time Jean had clutched my hand. When I looked down, indicating her hand clutching mine, he turned on his heel and walked out of the room. I received no further communication from him and no apology. Jean was in shock. What she said then was, "Cancer? Cancer? What did I do wrong? Has someone made a mistake?" Later, when I made a formal complaint to the BC College of Physicians and Surgeons about this physician, considering he was trained as a geriatric specialist, he did not acknowledge that this incident had even occurred. A day later he signed an order for Jean to be given loxapine *as needed,* against her own doctor's orders for no anti-psychotics, and wrote in her records his comment: *I know this patient well.*

Accompanied by her records from the care facility and this hospital's geriatric psychiatry unit, Jean was admitted to the medical ward, for palliative care, with a medical history that stated: *severe aggressive multi-infarct dementia.* She was to be treated for: *dehydration and pain management,* her primary diagnosis stated as: *dementia.*

Unbound

Unbound: undone, wounds not bound up ... released ... The morning after Jean's admission to palliative care on the medical ward, she was lying in bed in a room with three other women, two of whom alternately moaned, groaned loudly, shouted, yelled. The third remained completely silent. Jean reached for my arm, held on. She repeated the word "Cancer ... did someone make a mistake? What did I do wrong?" How could I reassure her? What could I say? "I don't know where to go. I don't know how. Where do I run to? Who is there?" Questions Jean had asked so often before. "Where is home?" she asked, "I want to go home now. I don't belong here." A multiplicity of meanings, for her, me. Nursing staff asked me if the morphine was controlling Jean's pain. Was it? Jean had a lifetime of hiding her pain. Similar to being poor, illness brought shame with it, denial. Now her body was breaking out, speaking for her. Morphine was initiated around the clock. She refused or spit out most oral doses, asking to be "left alone," and was given injections instead. Once the diuretic had some effect moving excess fluid out of her body, Jean was able to eat and drink a little more, became less delirious, more

Window in Jean's childhood.

clear, calm. She was uncomfortable lying down, likely due to the fluid gathering around her lungs, yet very tired sitting up and unable to support herself in a sitting position. Nursing records described Jean *wheeled around the halls in a geri-chair to increase environmental stimulation ... reaching out into space, appears to be trying to obtain some non-existent object. Episodes of restlessness ... transferred back to bed, very anxious on movement....* Staff here on the medical ward did not appear to have training that would provide them insight into Jean's situation, her need, not for environmental stimulation, but for a quiet, empathetic environment. There were signs and symptoms of understaffing and overwork in the impatience and restrained anger and hostility I had begun to feel from nursing staff. I attempted to explain Jean's need for quietness and requested a move to a private room I was told would be available the next day. Later that evening, September 18, after I had gone home for the night, Jean was described: *possibly hallucinating ... pointing to dark object in corner and saying "what is it?" ... appearing restless, confused, pointing her fingers in the air in front of writer, asking "how long they were planning to stay," when asked who "they" were patient replied "I do not know"....* Jean was moved the next morning to the private room, just become available, by a nurse who had demonstrated caring and acceptance of Jean.

Jean was assigned to this hospital's palliative team, which included a doctor who wrote his own profile of Jean, which I found only later in her records, in which he stated: *her unhappy childhood with violent father ... has had several unhappy relationships over her lifetime....* My first contact with this doctor occurred just outside Jean's hospital room, within her hearing, where he told me that he had read Jean's chart, commenting, "She must be a strong person to come through all she has." He then told me "he was from Manitoba too ... has read her history ... is aware of the trauma there...." I tried to draw him away down the hall, but he wanted to go in to see Jean, leaning his large, heavy-set frame on the bed table in front of her, his large bulk over her as she sat propped in her bed, in a nightgown, catheterized, an IV in her arm, struggling with everything that was being done to her. His face near hers, he asked Jean, who had never seen him before, "Do you remember when you were a little girl growing up on the farm in Manitoba?" Jean looked down at her hands, said in a quiet voice, almost to herself, "I've been a lot of places since then." A succinct, dignified response to an intrusive, unprofessional, and potentially very disturbing question that was a serious breach of Jean's right to privacy. She knew nothing of him and yet he was privy to very personal information about Jean. I was less polite, at least in my mind. I wanted to say, get out and leave my mother alone. Later, in 1995, I was given a copy of a letter this physician wrote to the College of Physicians and Surgeons, responding to my formal complaint regarding his actions, in which he stated, "I was simply trying to establish some contact with a demented, terminally ill patient."

Jean was subsequently quite uncomfortable with this doctor's visits. My daughter, when she arrived, noticed this as well. When I would ask him to speak with me regarding her, outside in the hall, he became annoyed. Later he began to put pressure on me for loxapine to be given to Jean "to make the nurses' job easier," and when I indicated this had been discontinued as it was contraindicated for Jean because of its toxic effects, he treated me as though I didn't know what I was talking about. Bullied me. I refused to be bullied, and when I described this interaction to Jean's own doctor, he indicated his recognition of this doctor's "bullish" tactics. I wondered why such a person would be involved in palliative care. This palliative doctor insisted unequivocally that the morphine sulphate Jean was being given in increasing doses would have no effect on her other than manage her pain, and, in earshot of Jean, told me "she doesn't look like she's dying." Immediately following Jean's encounter with this doctor and his question about "her childhood on the farm," Jean's records described her *very anxious, spitting out liquid morphine ... aggressive, pushing and pulling at nurse when morning care attempted.* Loxapine was then given for *aggressive behaviour.* Jean's own doctor apologized. Loxapine was then discontinued, and additional morphine injections were given Jean for increasing pain in her lower back.

The Swimmer Swims

Jean's doctor and I walked with Jean for a short distance in the hallway. She seemed stronger. Granular morphine had been given to me to mix in with Jean's meals. I told Jean her granddaughter was coming from Toronto to see her. Jean's eyes, her voice, unsure whether to believe it or not, wary, what does it mean? knowing what it means. It was a fall to honour Jean's passing, warm, dry, colours brilliant as a Manitoba Indian summer—golden evenings from her window, sunset and night appearing a little earlier each day. I was wheeling Jean in her chair onto the balcony next to her room, the balcony overlooking Vancouver, the north shore mountains, and across to where she had lived for the last twenty-four years since coming to Vancouver from Manitoba. Each day the sky remained infinitely blue, and an immature gull hung around crying to be fed. I took Jean to the balcony to catch the sun. The nurses had been pressing to have Jean moved out of her private room, which I was told was "needed for critical care," and "to send her to an extended care ward somewhere." Her doctor told me not to worry, there would be no problem with her staying where she was, advised me there was considerably more fluid gathering on her lungs, no point in taking it off, it would just come back.

When I was helping Jean to eat, drink, I had been asked to put not only morphine into whatever food she could manage, but an array of laxatives ordered by the geriatric specialist to, as he described it, *aggressively treat* narcotic-induced constipation. As morphine doses became more regular, Jean drifted, no longer agitated when cared for, quiet; out of pain, and spoke sometimes as though from another world. Occasionally a light came across her face, and a brief beautiful smile, different from the smiles we had begun to share over the last year, some wall finally breached. These smiles were mysterious, comforted me. Her breath, oceanic, labouring across my ear, as she coughed more, choked on her food, had increasing difficulty swallowing. Were her fears of what was happening to her subsumed by morphine? She asked less and less, but the questions still came, when she was conscious—"Where do I go? Where is home? How do I get there? I don't know where to run. Where do I go?" I would say, it's all right, don't worry, you'll be fine. We all feel this way. We don't know. Everyone is afraid. It's okay to be afraid. Then, instinctively, I said, go into who you are, go into your heart. You aren't just your body. Jean listened, said, "Yes," then said, "Thank you."

When Jean asked where her family was I told her in some way they would be with her. She asked for her mother and when I told her, as I had before, that they had all passed on before her and that she was the last one in her family, she was distressed. I told her then, but now there's me and your grandchildren, that her oldest grandson had just gotten engaged and that he would be coming soon, as well as her grand-daughter. She hadn't forgotten them. I kept telling her who I was. She knew me, and sometimes she didn't, but in some way knew and trusted me, even though she occasionally asked, "Fran used to come, where is she now?" It hurt me that her mind could give her that kind of loneliness and pain, but this may have been my perception, my own pain I was feeling. There was little I could do, except be with her, try to reassure, talk with her when she was conscious, hold her hand, a lot of the time, for her and for me, and touch her often. I brought in tapes of Celtic folk music to play softly and sat reading while Jean drifted. Her hearing appeared to be good, her eyesight, or rather her recognition of what she saw, fluctuated.

My daughter arrived and came with me to be with her grandmother.

We found Jean sleeping in her big recliner on wheels, facing the door—propped on one side with pillows and against the wall so she wouldn't fall over in any direction. My daughter said, "It's me, Gram," and Jean roused, said something like, "Oh yeah, sure" in a kind of disbelief, then realized it was her granddaughter, recognized her. "How are you?" she said, smiling. It was as though I saw Jean tall and erect again, striding to meet her granddaughter, the line below the skin.... When we left for a few hours, Jean got up out of her bed, pulled out her catheter, and was found by nursing staff later, after their considerable searching, sitting down in the corner of a stairwell at the end of a hallway. Later, during the evening, she appeared to be in pain and more morphine was given. Jean was noted to be asleep through the night. At 6:00 a.m. the next morning she was found kneeling on the floor. Her blood pressure was 210/100 and her pulse 100. By 8:00 p.m. she appeared to be in pain and was given morphine. Her blood pressure and pulse moderated somewhat. Her records indicated that during the period of her granddaughter's visit, Jean had recurrent periods of pain and agitation, which she did not express when we were with her, when Jean responded to everything her granddaughter said. In the next few days, when we took her out on the balcony and for short walks in the halls, it was as though Jean had her second wind. She stood with her granddaughter on the balcony looking out over the trees, beyond them the mountains, and blue of the Pacific Ocean rimming sky, and said, with a smile, a trace of apology in it, "I'm falling." We brought her back to her chair.

Suddenly Jean was gone again, drifting, unable to eat more than sips of vanilla ice cream, custards laced with morphine and laxatives. My daughter spent a day with Jean on her own. Nursing records indicate while her granddaughter was with her, Jean: *becomes very agitated on waking, grinding teeth, tone of voice harsh, facial gestures angry, describing with detail some negative/hostile past life experiences, unable to distract with usual distraction techniques, very involved in own thoughts, not alert to surroundings. Granddaughter is very anxious with patient's condition....* My daughter told me later that Jean had some really strange episodes while she spent the day with her. Also, that Jean told her, "I'm going to a beautiful place."

Jean's morphine orders were changed to what was called a *butterfly patch* in her right upper arm for morphine injection, a type of IV into which morphine can be syringed. Nursing notes indicated: *pharmacist concerned about new med. orders.* In order to deliver a regular pain-managing dose of morphine over a twenty-four-hour period, various methods were tried, including timed release. We were finding Jean sometimes semi-conscious, sometimes waving her hands and singing, spitting out food she didn't like, finally getting to express herself, reaching out for us. The week before, Jean was holding my hand, stroking me and my hair, holding her arms out to the nurses, hugging them. "I'm crazy," Jean said to us at one point and I told her, "If you are, we all are." Searching now for her brothers and mother, "where are the others?"

I had noticed since the latter weeks of her time in the geriatric psychiatry ward of this same hospital, and continuing in an increasing manner since, that Jean would jerk awake, then her body would continue jerking in a struggle to an upright sitting position, before jerking back into a sitting recline, as though struggling against both the weight of her lungs, and the pull back down of morphine. This happened both while in bed or in her chair. It was my daughter's last day. Jean, her eyes closed, occasionally calling out from her dreams, sipping only tiny amounts of mostly vanilla ice cream. Then she was with us again, opened her eyes, looked directly at my daughter and said, very clearly, "I'm tired, I'm sore, I'm old, I'm young," her parting words to her granddaughter.

Beyond Them

The fall weather remained golden and warm. We had been sitting outside with Jean each day, absorbing light and warmth. Once her granddaughter was gone, Jean seemed to need all her strength to breathe. She was sitting forward, rigid, trembling, shuddering, shuddering back, back, toward the pillow, the morphine taking her down against the weight of her lungs; then she would jerk, as though startled, wide-eyed and rigid, to go through it all again. Unable to lie back and needing to be propped up with pillows where she was, jerking, trembling as well, coughing and leaning forward to get her breath, she didn't seem to be able to sleep or rest. I had been approached a number of times about moving Jean to an extended care ward where she could be with others, "socializing." I was coming in from 8:00 a.m. to midnight to be with Jean, to let her know she was not alone, to assist her to eat and drink whatever she could, and to protect her. I watched, listened to the rhythm of her breathing, as I once must have from inside her, hearing now the rhythm of another birth, hers and mine, some transformation, but I didn't know what, that awaited us. Sometimes that smile, that light, came over her face....

I had a dream during this time, of a large and tall evergreen, a pine, in a forest, cut back, lopped off. There are some trees being logged around it and parts of myself in the form of children, perhaps waiting to be born, and suddenly the tree is whipping around in greater and greater circles, knocking everything down in its circumference. Debris is flying, devastation; will the tree uproot and fly away? Will I be hit? I woke up; found later, some old notes in my journal ... *senses ... amber sunlight, magenta a dark purplish red ... weaving sensation, thought and magic sound ...* I didn't know where this had come from, remembered amber is pine resin, said by the ancients to heal deafness, and that children represent a lost capacity to be in touch with the natural world, the primal state of being at home with, and to, feeling, sense, experience. The child was remembering her mother read to her ... *Four little foxes went to the fair ... saw some monkeys and elephants there ... rode and rode on the merry go round, four happier foxes couldn't be found....* remembering there were books and libraries, one tucked in behind the shoemakers below our rooms on Osborne Street, Jean encouraging me to read, discovering Winnie the Pooh, and laughing, and other worlds beyond the street and during the war, my mother folding bandages for the Red Cross, practising her first aid, arm slings and bandaging, on my father Saturday nights, Sunday afternoons, when he was home. And after he died, she found friends of his, one took me to baseball games at Osborne Stadium. He and his wife had no children. He was very kind, explained all the baseball strategy to me, but the game was too slow to hold my attention, the innings became endless, and I balked at going. Jean took care of it. The Christmas dinners with other friends, poor like us; teachers were not paid much then. Jean bought a second-hand piano so I could take lessons, didn't go out herself, but sent me to plays and musicals. I remember *King Lear, Little Women*, others, at the Playhouse in Winnipeg. She had sent me to summer camps, made sure I got to university, supporting me for what my summer wages, bursaries and scholarships didn't cover, for five long years. The child was tracing a mother's care, the bones of her character. The child and I were grieving our forgetfulness.

Jean was choking on food, suctioning of her throat required. A physiotherapist indicated, and wrote in Jean's records, that only jelled juice, sherbet, and very small sips of water would be safe. But the laxatives, thick and syrupy, kept coming, as well as crushed-up tablets with an unpleasant taste and difficult to mask. I was feeling the fear of what was coming. I touched Jean a lot, and told her often, it's me, Fran. She was very quiet, except for a deep cough, congestion, and her breathing. Jean was both rigid, unable to be moved backward into a reclining position, yet falling sideways so that she needed to be propped always with pillows into her chair and the chair pushed against the wall, otherwise her upper body would hang down over the arm of her chair. When the morphine took effect she drifted, jerking up, sometimes said, "Hello? who's there?" and jerking back down into semi-consciousness.

It was becoming difficult to hear what she said, when she did speak, but we did still talk, or I did mostly. Jean would say again she didn't know where to go. I talked about my father, her husband, and the walk he took with me just before he died. We were at West Hawk Lake, it was night and we were walking by the side of the highway and it was pitch black. We could see the stars. Every once in a while a car would come around the curving road and roar on past into the night. I don't remember exactly what I said to Jean, other than my father's words, telling me, as we looked up at the stars, that he didn't know what was out there, and that after he died I felt him near. Jean's eyes were open, looking at me. She was listening. I told her I wanted stay with her and take this journey as far as I could go with her. That yearling gull was crying out on the balcony. It came to watch me feed Jean when I brought her out to the balcony doorway to catch the evening light at suppertime, the bird watching us the whole time, shuffling away to hide behind the door when it saw me looking at it, then sidling back to watch again.

Sunsets those evenings were vivid in their clarity. Good weather for her journey. It had been the same when my father died, an Indian summer that October of his going. I wanted it to be different, the place of her going, but her room was a gift, quiet, windows looking out onto trees, sky, the light, birds, the sunsets. It was hard to know there was nothing I could do for her and there was so much we hadn't said to each other. So little time. I was uneasy about the morphine needed to manage Jean's pain. How much was too much?

The morning of September 28, when I arrived, Jean was sitting up in bed. A nurse was combing her hair. She smiled, I wasn't sure if the smile was perhaps for someone else, but it was a happy smile, and she said, "I'm back ... they are all taking care of me." The nurse told me very casually that "they almost lost her last night her respiration got so low."

No one had called me, although I had asked them to. Had she waited for me? That morning I told nursing staff I did not think it possible to give Jean the powdered and thick liquid laxatives I had been asked to give her for some time now, in with her food, as the physiotherapist had indicated to me that these should not be given. The nurse who had been combing Jean's hair earlier grabbed the spoon from my hand with which I had been feeding Jean some jelled juice, put several spoonfuls of sherbet into Jean's mouth, telling her to swallow it, then poured the laxative, approximately a quarter cup into Jean's mouth, followed by a mouthful of water. The nurse then turned to me and said, "There," and left the room. Fifteen minutes later Jean couldn't breathe and suction was needed to clear her throat. This same nurse then turned to me and said, "she should only have jelled juices."

During Jean's personal care that last day, one of the nurses complained loudly that Jean and "that other demented woman down the hall, what a load of trouble they are." I would have told that particular nurse to leave and not come back into Jean's room again; but for what had become an ever- present fear that later, when I was not there with her, Jean would somehow suffer for anything I said. One of the nurses laughed because Jean "wouldn't sit up." I was told I would need to sit in front of her and hold her in place while nurses left her room, Jean semi-conscious at this point, unable to hold her head up. We were left this way for half an hour. I could not let go of her, even to reach the call button, or Jean would have pitched forward onto the floor. On what would be the last day of her life, Jean, still very much intact within, knew what she felt. She heard and understood. Where should Jean be? Should a dying woman in palliative care not receive the same care as everyone else on this ward? Jean could not protect herself. When Jean did try to do so, in whatever way she could, when she could not find the words to speak the logic, the grammar of those who surrounded her, a story was told about her, but it was not hers.

Far Out to Sea

Jean's breathing laboured, then disappeared. Several seconds passed. She breathed again. These intervals of apnea, when Jean stoped breathing, had appeared with increasing frequency since Jean was sedated with Ativan. That last night, a fiery sunset, a vee of geese framed in Jean's window against the sky, their bellies glowing, something was different, Jean restless. At about 8:00 p.m. her whole body suddenly clenched. I knew something was *here*, something deep, different. I could see her heart beating on the surface of her chest, put my hand on the seam where her breast had been, and felt her heart, like a trapped bird, a powerful bird. I called a nurse, told her Jean's heart was racing, that she was in some kind of pain. Her heart kept pounding wildly against my hand. I could feel, hear it without my hand even near her chest. The nurse asked me, with what seemed to me like exasperation, "What is it you want me to do?" I forgot the paper I signed—*no heroic measures*; everything, was what I wanted to tell this nurse, expecting that would be her job. The shock of her words stopped mine. I want her to be comfortable, not in pain, I stammered, finally, to this nurse's back. Jean's doctor was called. When I spoke with him, he'd asked me to tell him what was happening, then said, "All that water weighing on her lungs, her heart has to work too hard, it's all ganging up on her," his voice, compassionate.

Morphine was injected through Jean's shoulder IV patch. She was restless, breathing heavily, obviously still in pain. I was holding her hand, lost in her hard breathing, her sighs and moans. Towards midnight I asked the nurse if Jean should have more morphine for what they called breakthrough pain. "Do you want her to have more?" was her response, leaving it up to me. I asked when Jean's next regular dose would be and was told "she can have as much as you want her to have." I requested Jean be given whatever was in the standing orders for her breakthrough pain, and later, Jean was then given her regular morphine injection around midnight. After this her restlessness stopped, she became still, except for laboured breaths to draw air into her drowning lungs through the congestion deep in her throat; and then the long silences when she didn't seem to breathe at all. The night nurse came in sporadically, told me this apnea was a dying sign, this apnea that had been with Jean since the psychiatric unit and all the drugs that were given to her there. I felt a shock of grief, breakthrough grief from whatever anaesthetized state I'd been in since the psychiatric ward; since how long? My heart knew the drugs imposed on Jean had brought her life to an end before it was her natural time to go.

The spaces between Jean's breathing grew longer. I was stroking her face and hair, found her hair, the back of her neck soaked, hot. I massaged her back and arms; her skin was so soft, unfamiliar, resonating oneness. Her hair had grown longer than I had ever seen, a soft silver streaked with auburn. I was remembering that song she sang when I was a child, *I dream of Jeannie with the light brown hair, born like a vapour on the soft summer air ...* these were the only words that came to me then. Jean cried breathing in, moaned. Was it pain, or was she exhausted, wanting it to be over?

"It's very near now," the nurse who answered my call said, explained the congestion in Jean's breathing was too far down to suction and she hadn't the strength to raise it up. Could Jean hear her words? My own distress intensified, mixed with relief she wouldn't have to endure this much longer. I tried to focus on stroking her face, her cheeks and forehead, arms, back, and shoulders, holding her hand. Such a rare and unfamiliar intimacy. I didn't know if I was doing this for Jean, if she wanted this, or not, or whether I was only comforting me. Would words help? It's okay, it's alright, it will be alright, I love you, I'm here ... slip from my mouth. Could she hear them, my voice, know that it was me? I had a sense that I was the frightened one, the scared child who couldn't let go. When I touched her face with a cool cloth, moistened her dry lips, Jean seemed to respond to this. Her eyes were open all the time. Did she see me? I wondered if her stare was on where she was going ... had she found the way as she struggled for air, with death? Once, maybe twice there was a possible smile. I was struck by its shyness, self-consciousness, almost embarrassment, neither of us used to this intensity, sharing it. I thought it said she knew I was there; more than involuntary muscles. Suddenly I wanted *heroic measures,* they said this was palliative care, that they would keep her comfortable and out of pain. Why weren't they doing all they could? Why have we been left alone? Why can't I stop this?

I could not stop this weeping that had, until Sam died, been so uncharacteristic of me, and stroking Jean. Remembered once bursting into tears like this, some time after my father died, when I found a little diary of his with his writing in faint pencil, hardly readable, perhaps from his time in the First World War. I cried then from a sudden realization I would never get know him as I got older, who he was, what he thought.

A team of nurses arrived to turn Jean in her bed, change her "diaper." Why did they keep calling it that? A larger version of a disposable diaper it was, but it was not for a child, an infant, it was for you, who had lived ninety years, who were both innocent and wise, perhaps wise enough to forgive this thoughtless callousness. I found myself torn between wanting Jean to be beyond their words, yet hearing mine. My presence was not acknowledged by this uniformed assault team who flipped on lights, moved Jean around on the bed, one more body to shift; placed pillows between her legs and around her back. She moaned and cried, heavy when they rolled her over, her arms and legs did not move, eyes like a newborn's staring up at the lights, wild look in them, struggling to stay with the light—or was it my fear that saw it this way, were you looking somewhere else, caught between two worlds? Finally the lights were flipped off again.

I know I was very angry with these people who kept coming in their professional uniforms, their armour; wordless, expressionless, their annoyance at my being there I could feel; turning Jean from one side to the other without speaking, flipping lights on, then off, leaving as they came, anonymous, uninvolved. One turned back to tell me, "I can't believe it, the night before, I was on and she was so feisty," the night I was told they "almost lost her." I thought of the morning after that night, when Jean was sitting up with a smile on her face, saying "I'm back" and I wondered if she'd come back for me, the child who couldn't let her go, in spite of those moments before her body clenched and her heart went wild, some hours ago, when I told her in my mind to follow her heart, it would take her where she needed to go, away from here. Prayed her heart would take her.

As dawn arrived, the apnea stopped, and Jean was breathing steadily; the congestion no longer audible when the nursing team arrived for their final turn of the night. I mentioned this, thinking Jean had rallied, made it through another night. It was 5:30 a.m. One nurse turned back to me as the others left the room. "She's fighting it," she said. "Just talk quietly in her ear and tell her it's all right to go." I had been telling her this one way or another all night and for days, but I stroked her arms and face and hair, kissed her face and wanted to lie down with her and hold her in my arms. I had fallen in love with her. I did lean over, then, close to her ear and told her it was alright to go, although if she could hear me she likely wasn't fooled. I told her that I loved her and, something very difficult for me, that I knew she loved me, that we would be together again. These are the words that came and I said them. Her mouth closed and she breathed through her nose a few times and suddenly a great wind came up out of her. Her eyes widened with surprise, an embarrassed look, and she closed her mouth. It happened two more times, the wind, trying to get out. True to her life she kept it in as much as she could until the last heave. Her spirit broke free, left her eyes.

I remember a physician quietly coming in and establishing a time of death—5:45 a.m., September 29, 1994. And a nurse telling me there would be a time when Jean would still be lingering and that I had an hour or so to be with her before they needed her room. What if you linger longer, I wondered, found myself speaking then directly to *you*. Shy now about touching you lying under covers, the light over your bed illuminating a smoothed face, the delicate bone structure, skin gentle over them; overnight I saw your face become like your mother Jane's and now your youthful beauty rests there. Hair silver and red. I have kissed your forehead and told you again I love you and will miss you, needing to say what has never been said until now. I was not prepared for the overwhelming grief, the sense the world would never be the same, nothing would ever be the same again; had never wept like that, perhaps something vestigial from the life of women, us, our fraught relationship, mother, daughter; fraught lives.

I called my son. He had planned to come to see his grandmother that day, and my older son had already booked a flight from Toronto to arrive in three days.

Jean's death certificate stated: *primary cause of death: dementia....* Crows came to the tree outside my bedroom window in the weeks after Jean died. Crows' wings dropping a feather weighing heart's rage. Who was, is accountable?

Greenness of Trees

Greenness of trees, tissue of heart. Jean's tree was planted into ground in January, 1995, four months after she died. Hard frosts since November had postponed this, and a cold January rain poured over us as we turned the final shovels of earth, spread and tucked it over buried roots, along with lavender crocus, their orange hearts already opened to sky. The tree is a linden, tall, slender, like her. We took pictures, the tree, my son, daughter-in-law, me....

Jean came to me in the weeks following her death, appeared in my mind. It was unexpected, I could not really explain how I saw her ... sitting in a chair, her winter coat on, smiling, at ease; another time walking a hallway of yellow walls that were not walls, a sense of lightness, that she was free, happy. I was surprised that it seemed to be in her former care facility. I woke up one night feeling a hand touch my cheek. It was from these I took solace. When she was cremated, I did not have a good feeling, knew then it was not what she wanted, that she hadn't been asked.

There was no mention in my journal at that time of the tree we planted, until one entry much later: *the tree, I have not written about it*

Jean, 1942.

yet, nor the grief that keeps coming up, or wants to, that I am unable to articulate; or the pain and fear of losing it, the grief, of being disabled, unable to feel. Grief had become a life companion, teacher, mentor ... shaping and reshaping the knowing, what the body tells. And for the child spiralling into that large, engulfing white flower that is *mother*, at its black centre a forest of yellow stamens she stands between, in the glow of their light, no longer trapped, grief will take her slipping down petals to see they are open, she can slide from there onto ground, become grass, water, wind and sky, look down on everything, see it all, lie on the shore, her sadness and fear of being alone dissolving ... she is water. She is life.

A crow came, remained beside the bench where I sat reading outside the library. The crows sat in the tree outside my window after Jean died. One of them hung upside down, eyed me as I wrote. They would sit in the branches of her linden tree and fly at my head sometimes when I approached, and I remembered again her story of pulling the tail feathers of a crow to make it stay the winter with her.

The crows were not there, July, 1998, Vancouver hot, dry, and the grass turning brown around Jean's tree, a Mongolian linden, used to growing in dry conditions, they told me, then putting out its delicately scented, creamy yellow blossoms. As I inhaled deeply to hold their fragrance, take it with me, my eye met a ladybug in the leaves, busily searching aphids. Ladybugs were a sign of good luck, goodness. I did not know where that came from. Perhaps I made it up. I took this as a gift, this chance meeting with a ladybug on my mother's tree, a gift from a devastated dignity, ninety years of walking her truth, her story in silence, protective silence, a dignity of strength, bearing the abuse that came early and late, the solitude of pain, and the courage to die with that dignity of beauty and grace in undignified circumstances.

Fall, 1999. This was the time to let her ashes go, to wind and sky, the scent of linden blossoms, which she loved, and the crows. I would take them to Winnipeg, put them into the ground where my father was buried. There was no marker there. I would have a marker made with both their names on it. Their breath in me my mother, the mother I grew in me to keep the flame going, the spark of life, and to know what can't be undone, can in time, or out of it, become the gift of an opened heart.

Epilogue: Missing Heartbeats

Unbound ... wounds not bound up .... Jean put up a massive struggle to survive what was being done to her. Whatever processes she was going through of short-term memory loss, after her heart fibrillated while being given a general anaesthetic during a mastectomy in June, 1988, it was indeed complex and little understood in its complexity by health care professionals, with the result that Jean's personality, her very character was ignored, denied, and pathologized by a system with predisposed attitudes to Jean that were widespread and took many forms. Among them: insensitivity, impatience, patronizing, condescension, callousness, invasion of her privacy, ignorance, fear, and hostility, resulting in subjective assumptions about her, her personality, what she was feeling. Labelling of Jean and interpreting her "behaviour" in negative terms allowed an assault on her body, her person to be rationalized, and her basic rights and needs betrayed.

Her natural, normal reactions to being labelled, depersonalized, and disrespected, not heard, when these occurred, was to act out what she could no longer verbalize quickly enough to meet the situation. Jean's natural defences, such as, for example, anxiety, were seen as a pathology, a clinical disease, which denied Jean the right to have feelings—a natural anger, grief caused by loss of control over her life, her sense of loss of self, and the right to process memories and unhealed feelings, to say no to drugs that made her sick, disabled her mind, her emotions. Jean had a right to respond to neglect, ignorance, and an abusive lack of insight from a health care system in which her feelings were no longer considered appropriate or allowed, or were considered "manifestations of psychotic behaviour." Rather than being persons with individual needs to be met, Jean and others in similar situations are seen as problems requiring pharmaceutical control. And for all too many who, like Jean, have kept wounded aspects of themselves silent, never speaking of trauma in early or later lives, now as they are in the last part of their journey, they are denied again the opportunity to speak, by a system of arbitrary authority, with no accountability and very limited tolerance for individual needs, differences, and above all individual choice. Caring according to needs, causing no harm, has been replaced with control of "disorder," maintained with the deep involvement of pharmaceutical agents and the industry behind them, as a "management" tool.

Acknowledgement, coming to terms with the past, no matter how late in life, is a human need. But words arranged in grammatical English sentences are not always adequate to articulate the flow of personal experience, feelings, thoughts, the underground stream of memory surfacing into consciousness, the stories circling and spiralling through our lives, particularly if someone is experiencing short-term memory impairment, and the loss of words that can accompany this. Jean's return to the world of her childhood, feeling the meaning of it, that life process, was seen in Jean as "crazy, nonsensical babbling, pathological," which provided a rationale for controlling her with drugs that would not only block essential life processes in her, but also produce their own toxicity, which was then seen as Jean's pathology, requiring even more drugs. Who will be an advocate for those who can't protect themselves? A private person always, in my memory, and she did not complain ever, so that when she began to have pain, she "denied it," as the system was so wont to describe. But this is how people who have lived through much hardship, as Jean had, cope. There is shame connected to illness, akin to that learned from poverty, which Jean knew all too well. She didn't deny illness, seeking medical help when needed. She knew poverty, had worked all her adult life until the age of seventy-nine, for very little money, denying herself holidays and other "extravagances" surviving early childhood trauma, two world wars, the great depression of the thirties, the loss of siblings and parents, her husband, becoming a widow raising a child alone on minimum wage, almost going blind with glaucoma and cataracts in later life. Then breast cancer at eighty-five and a heart fibrillation under anaesthetic during surgery that eventually took away her independence. But independence was how Jean had survived her life—a simple, quiet life.

As a child she walked through prairie fields from her farm home to school in town. She walked downtown to work in Winnipeg, to the library, walked in Vancouver even when she was almost blinded by cataracts and glaucoma, going by feel, and continued walking once her eyesight was restored. It was integral to her life. Suddenly cut off from this lifetime of walking in a care facility, Jean was described as "wandering and restless" when she walked in the halls. The body's natural way of restoring balance, of stimulating the natural flow of chemical information that restores homeostasis, balance, the good feelings we need to cope each day, in Jean was seen as something negative, *a risk to elope,* a symptom of disorder. But it was not Jean who was disordered, in this absence of the loving-kindness of common sense. Rare were the moments when I observed Jean touched or spoken to in a loving way.

To orient ourselves, according to the dictionary, is to identify our position with regard to the points of a compass; to orient a map is to place it so that its bearings correspond with one's own; to face or move towards a certain direction. By orienteering we find our way across rough and unfamiliar country by map and compass. Jean's map had bearings that corresponded to her own, and similarly her internal compass. When Jane, my grandmother, gave birth to her, three years earlier Marconi had radiotelegraphed across the Atlantic, and within three years of her birth the vacuum tube was invented. By the time Jean was eleven, voice could be transmitted by radio, the first commercial radio on air when she was sixteen. Yet, from the time she was a child, Jean learned silence.

Loose Pages

Unbound ... not held accountable.... After Jean's death, I could not continue writing the initial draft of the novel funded by the Canada Council. I wanted my mother's records, to understand why this had happened to her, and those responsible held accountable. The foundation of any system is necessarily individual accountability. Without personal responsibility and acknowledgement of errors, harm done, there is no change possible, individual or systemic.

From January 1995, when I began requesting Jean's records from various institutions, through freedom of information legislation, until 1999, I accumulated a huge file of correspondence and reports detailing my dance with the bureaucracy that became a very long, very slow shuffle, as the music shifted, wove its subtle rhythms, sliding and gliding through different partners, shades, nuances of tone, becoming more and more distant, a murmur, slippage....

The Ministry of Health in BC had investigated, in response to my submission based on Jean's records, and indicated to me that no one was found to be at fault, and stated that Jean received "adequate care," in spite of their finding the care facility's records "incomplete, inaccurate and subjective," and recommending the facility improve its method of keeping records, its training of staff in their approaches to residents. Their letter to me at the conclusion of their investigation ended by saying that the care facility "met the requirements of the legislation" and they could assure me that the Ministry of Health "continues working to ensure residents receive quality care." The British Columbia Inter-Ministry Committee On Elder Abuse had already adopted their Principles and Procedures and Protocols for Elder Abuse (1992), which defined abuse in a number of situations, among which are the following: over-medication, untreated medical problems, active neglect, where there is intentional withholding of care, and passive neglect, due to lack of experience, information, or ability. My word, any evidence I brought forward, was not considered. I discovered that, in every instance, only the various institutional records kept on Jean were considered reliable evidence on which to base an assessment of her care, despite various findings of "incomplete, inaccurate and unprofessional record-keeping" at the care facility. Two nurses at the care facility were "verbally reprimanded," but no formal disciplinary action was be taken because, in the words of the RNABC (Registered Nurses Association of BC), the *problem is systemic*.

The College of Physicians and Surgeons of BC, after an in-camera review, absolved all medical and psychiatric staff named in my formal complaint—the head of the geriatric psychiatry unit, the psychiatrist assigned to Jean, and her supervisor, and, as well, the geriatric specialist and palliative care physician—of any accountability in the their treatment of Jean and suggested I lacked an understanding of her situation. The Ombudsman's Office of BC requested the College provide me with a more comprehensive report. I was then sent another, just as inaccurate and vague, but written as though I might be having trouble understanding anything other than very simple sentences. I was able to acquire, from the College, copies of letters of response to the College's review from the various psychiatrists and medical doctors I had named in my formal complaint. All, in their letters, claimed "no recollection of events." The senior psychiatrist supervising the young resident psychiatrist assigned to Jean, and who did not make himself known to me at any time while Jean was under his supervision, suggested in his letter that I had a history as a troublemaker, referring to Jean's encounter, in 1991, while she was still living in her home, with the geriatric assessment unit and their discharge report, referred to earlier in the book.

The Office of the Ombudsman in BC, in 1999, attempted to change legislation to allow immediate family members of individuals whose care was being investigated by the College of Physicians and Surgeons, to have access to the minutes of in-camera meetings. This was not successful at that time.

In the end the bureaucracy protected its own, danced me off the edge and into the deeps of *no one's fault.*

Appendix

Sources & Additional Information
Information regarding drugs, their use and effects, including side and adverse effects, recommended dosages, etc., was taken from *The Compendium of Pharmaceuticals and Specialties* (33rd edition, 1998), *The Essential Guide to Prescription Drugs,* James J. Rybacki, Pharm D., and James W. Long, M.D., Goodman & Gillman's *The Pharmalogical Basis of Therapeutics,* ninth edition, and American Medical Association Drug Evaluations 1995, *The Merck Manual of Geriatrics* 1998, *Drug Facts and Comparisons, Psychotropic Drug Fast Facts, Handbook of Psychiatric Drug Therapy.*

Side effects are defined in this literature as those effects that are likely to accompany the use of any particular drug; Adverse effects described as those that have been observed, that may pertain to individual sensitivity, age, other factors, overdosage, drug interactions, etc.

Other sources:
Biological Psychiatry, 1991
La Presse Medicale, 1986
Brain Disabling Treatments in Psychiatry, Peter R. Breggin, M.D.

Islands in a Gap
Page 5: Jean's records indicated that for the general anaesthesia during her mastectomy surgery, when she experienced heart fibrillation, the following drugs were used:

Thio Pental Sodium (Pentothal) is a fast-acting IV barbiturate. Individual response to this drug is so varied that it must be carefully titrated against age, sex, and body weight. Slow, incremental injection is recommended, if at all, in the case of untreated hypertension, to minimize respiratory depression and the possibility of overdose. Pulse should remain normal, increase slightly and return to normal. Adverse effects are listed as cardiac arrhythmias and tachycardias (irregular and elevated heart rhythm) among others. Arrhythmias may appear if carbon dioxide level is elevated but they are uncommon with adequate ventilation. They are especially likely to occur if the heart muscle has been sensitized by inhalation of halogenated anaesthetics such as isoflurane, which was administered to Jean.

The incidence of adverse effects is the principal factor that now determines the acceptability of a general anaesthetic agent. Induction of anaesthesia by isoflurane is assisted by the injection of Pentothal and the use of enhancing (adjuvant) drugs, analgesics, muscle relaxants, to reduce the dose of volatile anaesthetic. By using a combination of drugs a balancing effect is sought for and a reduction in the overall dosage of each drug used. Isoflurane has the effect of increasing the heart rate and the action of muscle relaxant agents. Isoflurane also depresses respiration, this action exacerbated by pre-medications with opioids (analgesics related to morphine) such as fentanyl (80x more potent than morphine). Isoflurane also can stimulate airway reflexes, resulting in an increase in secretions, coughing and laryngospasm. Pre-anaesthetic medication and induction of anaesthesia with Thiopental is used in an attempt to reduce these effects.

Geriatric literature indicates many anaesthetists now avoid pre-operative sedation for aging individuals because it further reduces the already compromised ventilatory response to hypoxia and hypercapnia, that is, the imbalance of oxygen and carbon dioxide within the body that becomes a source of heart arrhythmias during anaesthesia. In Jean's case, Serax (oxazepam) was used as pre-anaesthetic and as an additional intravenous sedative during her surgery. Serax, also known as oxazepam is one of the family of benzodiazepines which are anxiolytics, or tranquilizers, which depress the central nervous system. Serax, pharmacology literature indicates, has a half-life of 3 to 21 hours and is used in symptomatic relief of manifest anxiety and tension state in psychoneurotic patients. It is noted that this drug is not usually indicated for use with anxiety or tension associated with everyday life and contraindicated in patients with a previous sensitivity and with glaucoma, a condition pre-existent in Jean for the past two decades. Jean's records from 1984 surgery would have been useful had it contained this indication, assuming these earlier records would be checked.

The recommended dosage of Serax (oxazepam) for those over 60 is 5 mg once or twice a day, as tolerated, treatment to be initiated by the lowest dosage and increased gradually as needed and tolerated to avoid over-sedation and neurological impairment, such as memory loss. While the dosage given Jean was not ongoing, and involved two individual dosages prior to and post-surgery, it was 15-30 mg, not including what she received intravenously during her surgery. If any of these benzodiazepines are given concurrently with analgesics, such as fentanyl, also given to Jean, the combination may result in prolonged depression of respiratory response to lowered oxygen and increased carbon dioxide levels. Extreme caution is recommended.

The analgesic fentanyl, a synthetic opioid analgesic 80 times more potent than morphine, was given to Jean by injection during surgery. Fentanyl has adverse effects related to heart arrhythmias and rapid pulse. Changes in heart rate, notably tachycardia, or rapid heart rate and palpitations, are also associated with atropine, another IV drug given Jean during her surgery. Atropine (a belladonna alkaloid) blocks the stimulatory action of acetylcholine and produces muscle relaxation at sites like the bladder, intestine, and bronchi, and dries up secretions in the mouth and lungs during general anaesthesia. Adequate doses of atropine can abolish many types of reflex vagal cardiac slowing (asystole) from, for example, irritant vapours such as inhaled during anaesthesia, and also prevents or abruptly abolishes cardiac slowing (asystole) and broncho-constriction caused by acetylcholinesterase inhibitors such as neostigmine, which was also administered to Jean during her surgery. Pharmacological literature indicates: these drugs (neostigmine) have "received extensive application as toxic agents in the form of agricultural insecticides and potential chemical warfare nerve gases...nevertheless several members of this class of compounds are widely used as therapeutic agents...." Too high a dose results in an increase in heart rate as well as central nervous system depression in which hypoxemia, too low a concentration of oxygen, is a major factor.

Aside from digoxin and Inderal, which were used to counteract the fibrillation of Jean's heart while under anaesthesia, the other IV drug used during her surgery was the muscle relaxant pancuronium, a neuromuscular blocking agent similar to the paralytic action of curare to the junction between nerve and muscle. Persistence of such blockage and difficulty with complete reversal of this action is a feature of the more potent long-acting pancuronium, which shows virtually no histamine release but results in vagal blockage and tachycardia. Neostigmine is used subordinately to reverse or decrease the effect of pancuronium blockage and atropine as an antagonist to neostigmine, but atropine can enhance the effects of the neuromuscular blockers, such as pancuronium, particularly in the early stages of administration. Isoflurane and pancuronium react to increase each other's effect. Digoxin and Inderal were used intravenously when Jean's heart began to fibrillate after being given all of these agents of anaesthesia.

Inderal is used for tachyarrhythmias due to excessive catecholamine action (the physiological and metabolic responses that follow stimulation of sympathetic nerves in response to stress during anaesthesia, resulting in an increased heart rate and its force of contraction). Extreme caution is required in administration of Inderal in those with non-allergic bronchospasm, such as emphysema. Among other adverse effects are those to the central nervous system: dizziness, weakness, insomnia, anorexia, anxiety, mental depression, poor concentration, reversible amnesia and catatonia, hallucinations, paraesthesia, and incoordination.

Cimitidine, a histamine blocking agent given to Jean prior to surgery, is used to prevent aspiration pneumonitis caused by anaesthesia, and has among its possible adverse effects abnormal heart rhythm changes and tachycardia. The dosage for those over 60 should be 150 mg, half the normal adult dose. Her chart indicates Jean was given 300 mg prior to her surgery. Cimitidine decreases diazepam (benzodiazepine) clearance resulting in a more pronounced and prolonged sedation.

The metoclopramide (Maxeran) given to Jean prior to surgery to reduce postoperative vomiting, is contraindicated for those with a known sensitivity to it. Significant extrapyramidal reactions, those affecting motor control in the brain, can occur at what are considered therapeutic doses. The elderly are particularly vulnerable to these disabling effects. Therapeutic dosages are calculated from lean body weight, the total adult daily dose equivalent to .5 mg x kg of body weight. Jean's weight indicated a normal adult dosage of 5 mg at any one dose. Her age suggests a further reduction would be required. She was given 10 mg prior to surgery. Among other possible adverse effects noted for metoclopramide are neuroleptic malignant syndrome (see end note 2., Light on an Outspread Wing) and abnormal heartbeat.

Page 7: An alternate procedure to the modified radical mastectomy Jean underwent in 1988 is described in the BC Cancer Control Agency's literature as a *partial mastectomy or wide lumpectomy*, considered appropriate where the tumour is *less than 4cm. and singly focussed*. In this procedure, which can be done *with the use of local rather than a general anaesthesia, the tumour and a safety zone of surrounding normal tissue is removed, combined with axillary node dissection....* This refers to the removal of some, or all neighbouring lymph nodes so that these may be tested for the presence of invasive cancer—a procedure the agency describes in their literature as *still the most powerful prediction of the need for adjuvant (additional) therapy.*

The protocols set up by the Cancer Control Agency of BC state that such a partial mastectomy can be considered where the tumour is *sufficiently small in size in relation to the rest of the breast so that a wide local incision with a margin of normal tissue will leave a reasonable cosmetic result... radiology on the breast and possibly to the axilla is required....* These protocols have been established by the Breast Tumour Group, made up of surgeons (of whom Jean's surgeon was one), specialists in radiation and medical oncology, diagnostic radiology, epidemiology and pathology. The protocols describe what determines which procedure will be chosen. Jean's surgery, modified radical mastectomy, is the treatment of choice if any of the following criteria apply: *a multi-focal tumour is present in the breast, or its size such that removal of the primary tumour with an adequate margin of normal tissue would lead to considerable distortion of the breast, or if radiation therapy cannot be used in follow-up, for instance, because of pre-existing significant lung disease, or if the patient is elderly...since modified radical mastectomy is always easier on the patient than a partial mastectomy, node dissection and radiation therapy....*The final consideration is availability of follow-up.

LIGHT ON AN OUTSPREAD WING

Page 9: the anti-psychotic Stemetil was used, according to Jean's records, as an anti-nausea agent after her lens implant surgery in 1984 and is described in the literature with possible benefits of effective control of acute mental disorders, nausea and vomiting, and relief of anxiety and nervous tension. It is contraindicated where there is cancer of the breast ... this drug is also contraindicated in those over 60, for non-psychiatric use for which other drugs are available, as the aging are especially prone to develop adverse effects from anti-psychotic drugs. Adverse effects of Stemetil that are dose related or those due to individual sensitivity include: dystonias (movement disorders), as well as weakness, insomnia, agitation, impaired day and night vision. Agitation is one of the effects, and an indication of an overdosage. The single dose recommended for those under 60 is 5-10 mg Ten mg is the suggested starting individual psychiatric dose for those under 60. Jean at eighty years of age, was given 7.5 mg of Stemetil. Caution is advised using this drug in the presence of glaucoma. Tylenol with codeine interacts with anti-psychotics such as Stemetil, and with sedatives oxazepam and diazepam to further depress central nervous system activity. Among the most frequently observed adverse effects are nausea and vomiting, allergic effects, dysphoria or euphoria and abdominal pain. The caffeine component can cause nausea, headache, and insomnia.

Following administration of the Stemetil and Tylenol with codeine, nurses' shift reports indicated Jean: *assisted up walking a short distance, appearing vague at times, and resting in bed. feeling better, eating and caring for herself, no stated complaints.* But by 3:00 a.m. of the next day, nursing shift notes indicated a number of adverse effects that in the literature are related to Stemitil: *agitated and very testy since another patient was brought into the room. Each attempt to pacify rejected and evidently forgotten but each imagined grievance remembered vividly and recited verbatim. Wants nurse to stop coming into her room and she doesn't care about the other person who has not right to be in "my" room.* And at 6:00 a.m.: *did not remember any man in her room and didn't want me to come near her. Had no memory of me at all despite a half dozen previous meetings tonight.* The next day, 12:30 p.m., July 6, Jean's records indicate: *discharged from hospital, left walking accompanied by her daughter.*

Adverse effects from prescribed medications were not noted in Jean's records. Paradoxical (reverse) and rebound effects from introducing neuroleptics (Stemetil is of this class of drugs) and then withdrawing them can mimic psychosis and these rebound effects when seen, pharmacological literature states, indicate the possibility of neurological impairment. Why was Jean given Stemetil at all, when by 5:00 a.m. prior to being given Stemetil and Tylenol with codeine, nursing records indicate: *pt. less agitated-nausea less, refusing analgesic—states no pain.* The very oddity of the episode from 3:00 to 6:00 a.m. on July 6, prior to Jean leaving hospital, would indicate an adverse reaction to Stemetil with possible neurologically harmful effects.

Out of Time

Page 107: Delirium is characterized by an altered state of consciousness, confusion, distractibility, disorientation, disordered thinking and memory, defective perception (illusions and hallucinations) prominent hyperactivity, agitation and autonomic nervous system overactivity, as defined in *Stedman's Medical Dictionary*. Deliriant, a toxic substance that causes delirium.

Page: 107: Excerpt from a letter from the care facility, confirming the decision to give Jean risperidone: *This letter serves to summarize the meeting that took place on May 4, at (the facility) regarding your mother ... has been diagnosed to have Multi-infarct Dementia/Chronic Organic Brain Syndrome. Due to this progressively degenerative disease process the behaviours demonstrated by those individuals are specific. The behaviours presented by her are: isolativeness, paranoia, unpredictable agitated times that lead to unprovoked aggression. The staff have continued to observe, care for her present needs and have documented her behaviours and responses. Due to her present nature and on what we discussed throughout the meeting, it was genuine feeling by all present that we all recognize to meet the best quality of life for Jean at her present home. We also agree that a low dose of medication given to her regularly could possibly assist her in controlling behaviours. Nursing will be documenting her progress and the results of this medical treatment. Along with myself ... Social worker ... BC Community Liaison and (her doctor) are available for consultation. Again we appreciate all the time and energy you have given out voluntarily to assist us in your mother's personal care.*